Praise for

EVERYDAY *Savior*

"In order to keep our baptismal covenant to 'always remember Him' (Moroni 5:2), we need to develop a genuine and deep relationship with Christ that will enable Him to be an Everyday Savior for us. As Brother Raleigh illustrates in his book, 'always remembering Him' means regularly recognizing His hand in our daily lives. He writes, 'One of the greatest skills we can develop in mortality is the ability to look at our life experiences and see the lessons that . . . will ultimately bring the Savior more clearly into view. . . . If we will strive to find the lesson in our own experiences, we will come to see His hand in our daily lives.' As we develop that awareness that Christ is intimately involved in the day-to-day details, it will surely fill our lives with power and give us the strength to endure all things."

—ALONZO L. GASKILL, best-selling author of *Sacred Symbols* and professor of Church history and doctrine at Brigham Young University

Everyday *Savior*

Recognizing *His Hand* in *Your* Daily Life

Winn Raleigh

CFI
An imprint of Cedar Fort, Inc.
Springville, Utah

ISBN 13: 978-1-4621-2312-4

Published by CFI, an imprint of Cedar Fort, Inc.
2373 W. 700 S., Springville, UT 84663
Distributed by Cedar Fort, Inc., www.cedarfort.com

LIBRARY OF CONGRESS CATALOGING-IN-PUBLICATION DATA

Names: Raleigh, Winn, 1955- author.
Title: Everyday Savior : recognizing His hand in your daily life / Winn Raleigh.
Description: Springville, Utah : CFI, an imprint of Cedar Fort, Inc., [2019] | Includes bibliographical references and index.
Identifiers: LCCN 2018047972 (print) | LCCN 2018053364 (ebook) | ISBN 9781462130016 (epub, pdf, mobi) | ISBN 9781462123124 (perfect bound : alk. paper)
Subjects: LCSH: Christian life--Mormon authors. | Church of Jesus Christ of Latter-day Saints--Doctrines. | Mormon Church--Doctrines.
Classification: LCC BX8656 (ebook) | LCC BX8656 .R35 2019 (print) | DDC 248.4/89332--dc23
LC record available at https://lccn.loc.gov/2018047972

Cover design by Jeff Harvey

Edited by Hali Bird and Sydnee Hyer
Typeset by Kaitlin Barwick

Printed in the United States of America

10 9 8 7 6 5 4 3 2 1

Printed on acid-free paper

TO MY FAMILY AND FRIENDS

who have tirelessly listened to my stories with interest and appreciation

Contents

INTRODUCTION

Wisdom is knowing someone has gone before us and has endured

One of the most important legacies a person can pass on to future generations is memories of the past, rich with experience. This kind of richness can be found in the lives of those who have learned to share selflessly with others. These golden threads of experience weave a tapestry that warms the soul with wisdom gained from a life well lived.

Developing this kind of wisdom begins with learning from those who have gone before us and have marked the way. The following analogy illustrates this thought.

> *In a time far removed from the modern age, there lived a great Indian chief, who was a great example of wisdom and courage to his people. This chief had a young son who would one day succeed him as the tribal leader if he proved himself worthy. A tribal custom required that a young boy who had reached the age of accountability be given a test to prove his manhood and show his leadership ability.*
>
> *On the appointed day, the chieftain-father approached his son and told him that he must prove himself worthy to those he would one day lead. He told the boy if he could pass the difficult test, he would no longer be counted a boy but take his place as a young man within the tribe. The boy eagerly accepted, and early the following morning the journey began.*
>
> *After traveling days through the searing heat of the desert, they arrived at the base of a large rocky mountain with peaks that soared*

toward heaven. It was there that the father placed before his son the great test: "If you will climb to the top of this mountain, at its peak you will find your manhood. You will discover courage, gratitude, humility, and wisdom."

The boy, already exhausted from the journey, thought this was an impossible task to accomplish. The father, sensing the anxiety in his son, gently placed his hand upon the boy's head and assured him that he would never offer a task that he himself would not undertake. Taking courage from his father's words, the boy slowly began to ascend the mighty mountain. The climb toward the peak was long and dangerous, and the sharp rocks cut and bruised the boy as he moved. Often, the boy wanted to quit as frustration took control, but his father's words fueled his desire to continue, and he labored slowly and painfully upward until he finally reached the peak. The boy was exhausted but felt exhilaration once he realized what he had done, and it was there that he discovered the meaning of maturity, just as his father had promised.

The boy's chest swelled with pride for having found the ***courage*** *to overcome his wounds. The realization that he could not have done it alone gave birth to sincere* ***gratitude*** *for help from a higher source. As he bowed his head in* ***humility*** *to give thanks for the strength to complete the test, he noticed at his feet the markings of someone who had been there before him—his father. It was at that moment that he gained a measure of* ***wisdom*** *as he realized that he was never alone in his journey.*

The moral of this story mirrors our experience here in mortality; we are not alone in our journey here. No matter how impossible tasks may seem, no matter how frustrating life may be, or even how often our experiences may wound us, there has always been someone who has gone before us. And further still, there is one individual who has gone before us all, enduring all things in our behalf.

This knowledge can help soften the harshness of life, and fortunately for us, the Lord has perfectly endured this journey we call mortality and has pointed out the safest course for us to follow. There need be no mystery to our journey here, and confidence waxes strong in the knowledge that God the Father, and His Son Jesus

Christ, have never exacted from man any act of obedience or sacrifice that They have not acquiesced to. Further comfort is derived from Lorenzo Snow's aphorism of Joseph Smith's teaching:

> As man now is, God once was. As God is now, so man may be. (King Follett discourse, by Joseph Smith the Prophet. See *The Vision*, 17–18)

This thought is in complete harmony with the Lord's own enlightening statement of truth:

> Verily, verily, I say unto you, The Son can do nothing of himself, but what he seeth the Father do: for what things soever he doeth, these also doeth the son likewise. (John 5:19)

Our Heavenly Father and His Son understand our mortal experience because Their knowledge has been reared from experience. As a result, Their counsel and commandments are given with wisdom born of a selfless concern for others.

In my own life, fatherly wisdom taught me that during difficult times, we must look at God's foreknowledge and wisdom from a different point of view than does the natural man. When adversity knocks, we often wonder why such an ugly stranger intrudes in our lives, particularly while we are striving to serve faithfully where we stand and remain obedient to God's commandments. Wisdom whispers, however, that we find comfort and peace in knowing that because we are doing what is right, we are entitled to receive divine help from a loving eternal parent who understands our personal situation. What a difference perspective can bring! Divine perspective unleashes a healing balm that restores strength and brings endurance in our lives.

The exemplary life of the Lord was a panoramic view of wisdom, knowledge, and the power of godliness. Scriptures further reveal the characteristics of deity that are required for man's safest ascent of the rocky peaks of mortality. Eternal perspectives provide a clearer view of what exists beyond—God's life.

To attain such eternal quarters, the Lord has established His church and gospel upon the earth to give us a sure foothold while we climb ever upward in our own quest to reach the top.

One of the more interesting ways the Lord helps us gain wisdom in this life is through our own unique experiences that can teach us life lessons. When we learn to see the lessons in our daily lives, we come to see the Lord more clearly. I love what is taught to Moses in the Pearl of Great Price about Jesus Christ and His creations:

> And behold, all things have their likeness, and all things are created and made to bear record of me, both things which are temporal, and things which are spiritual; things which are in the heavens above, and things which are on the earth, and things which are in the earth, and things which are under the earth, both above and beneath: all things bear record of me. (Moses 6:63)

When we understand that all things bear witness of Christ, then we know we can find Him more clearly in our daily lives through experiences we have. One of the greatest skills we can develop in mortality is the ability to look at our life experiences and see the lessons that we can learn from, lessons that will ultimately bring the Savior more clearly into view. This expanded view will help us find our way through this mortal experience and come closer to reaching our godly potential. I know that Christ is an everyday Savior, and if we will strive to find the lessons in our own experiences, we will come to see His hand in our daily lives. May God bless you on your important journey here, to see and acknowledge the Lord's hand in your life every day.

1

A Clever License Plate

Avoiding the appearance of evil or wrongdoing

At forty-two years old, I made a critical career change in my life that required us to move to Los Angeles County. Being raised in San Diego, this was a challenge for us because we "619" people are raised to despise Los Angeles. We relocated to a beautiful valley called Santa Clarita in the hills above the San Fernando Valley. We fell in love with it immediately for several reasons. First of all, it had four seasons, unlike San Diego, and we loved the temperature changes and the colors. Secondly, it was so family-oriented there, with wonderful paseos to walk and ride on, lots of kids, and the beautiful surroundings—we loved living there. It was so different from the L.A. basin, being up in elevation and surrounded by the most beautiful and unusual mountains. It was such a great feeling to drive home every day into those mountains and the valley of Santa Clarita.

I worked in the basin covering the San Fernando Valley, and we quickly learned that in Los Angeles, you don't measure travel by distance; you measure by time. You could live thirty miles from a destination and it could take you sixty to ninety minutes to get there. On those freeway commutes, I would try to focus on something other than my frustration with being stuck in a perpetual traffic jam. I started to look at license plates and where people were from. Los Angeles is a melting pot, and there are always interesting out-of-state plates to look at. I would think about what it was like there, the different accents, their culture and food choices, home prices. I looked at the styles of cars, their cost, and the people driving the cars—anything to keep me occupied.

One morning, while driving to work, I happened to look in my rearview mirror and noticed a car weaving in and out of lanes, trying to get an edge on the slow traffic. I was watching a driver that was manifesting the impatience the rest of us were feeling. As the car worked its way through traffic and passed by me in another lane, I saw that the driver was a young teenage girl driving a red convertible sports car. I started to feel some irritation at her impatient driving. I believe it is the impatient people constantly changing lanes, causing people to brake, that ultimately slow things down and often bring the traffic to a grind.

As if to prove my point, she got stuck in a lane that slowed her down so that I caught up with her, and as I was justifying my critical judgment of her driving skills, I noticed something interesting. What caught my attention was the license plate. It read, "WHY GO 55." Yes, at one point in history the maximum speed limit on the freeways was fifty-five miles an hour—no wonder it took us so darn long to get anywhere. Today, it seems to be a phenomenon that whatever the posted speed limit is, everyone is expected to go ten to twenty miles an hour faster, and if you don't, you tick everyone off except the few others who *do* go the speed limit. Back in the "55" days, most everyone went the speed limit, even if you had the open road to go faster.

My first reaction was one of amusement for a clever personalized license plate. But as I continued to think about the intended message, amusement turned to interest. What might be the potential ramifications of that seemingly harmless license plate? I decided to ask a friend, who was a police officer, some questions: "What kind of cars are most frequently pulled over for speeding?" He replied, "Sporty-looking cars." I then asked, "What colors stand out most?"

He responded, "Bright colors." I inquired why that would make a difference, and he explained that the bright colors enhance the speed of the car—they appear faster than other cars. Remember, back then radar guns were used but were often not that accurate, so sight and experience were the determining factors when it came to speed. I finally asked a question that would not be politically correct today: "What part of the population seems to be pulled over more than most?" He quickly responded, "Teenagers." I don't know if that info fits every city, but it sounded right based upon my own observations. It is interesting to me that we often see in others what we did not see in ourselves when we were that age. For us older folk, I'm sure we caused many others frustration by our own poor driving skills when we were young.

As I reflected upon the young lady driving the bright-red sports car, I realized she was profiled as an individual who was susceptible to being pulled over more than the average driver. To make her situation even more tenuous, she increased her odds of attention by attaching a message to her car that boasted of open defiance for the speed limit. Was she being cute or careless?

I think at times we do things without much forethought, simply because it entertains us or gets a chuckle from others. I know I have often said or done things for amusement and then wished I hadn't said or done that.

What is interesting to consider is the fact that she may never break the speed limit, as unlikely as that may be, and she still may be pulled over more than the average driver. Why? Because she has intentionally put herself in a position of vulnerability. Think about that for a moment. Don't we all at times make ourselves a little more vulnerable by choices we make that are simply intended to be amusing in some way, or because we may be a little impatient or just flat-out selfish? If we take honest introspection of our own lives, we may find we hang plates of defiance on ourselves and don't realize it. Yet when consequences arise from those declarations, we see them as unfair to us, when we don't have the right to be upset because we caused it, or at the very least put eventual consequences into play.

In thinking about this young lady, the intended message of amusement, "WHY GO 55," may not even be the real message there. It isn't about how fast she goes or intends to go, it is the perceived description of that individual in the minds of others that matters. The scriptures reveal a clearer message to spiritually minded individuals:

> Abstain from all appearance of evil. (1 Thess. 5:22)

Today, I would add the word "wrongdoing" as well. Most of us are not out to do evil or even appear to be doing evil. But it is much easier in today's world to see in others what appears to be wrongdoing, even when it isn't. The key words in the above passage are "*all appearance.*" The word "all" means anything that may appear in any way to be trouble, regardless of how innocent the nature of the act may be. The perception of others is important. Is this fair? It is if we understand the influence we can have for good or bad upon others solely based upon their perceptions of us.

Even if the perception is not real or accurate, it does determine our level of influence. This requires that we at times sacrifice things that may be innocent but may not *appear* to be innocent. For instance, coming out of a liquor store after midnight with a paper bag of milk in it may not be a good idea, especially for a Word of Wisdom–keeping Latter-day Saint. But it is only milk in the bag, you say! That is not what it would look like to others who know us and may happen to drive by at an opportune time to see us coming out of a liquor store late at night. Unfortunately, some will see you with a bag of booze even though it is just milk. That is why perception is key. Some will say, "Who cares what others think? All that really matters is what I think, and I know I am not doing anything wrong." Let me share an example that is relevant to our youth today.

Some of our own innocent young people attend parties where the Word of Wisdom and morality are abused openly, and yet they rationalize being there as okay because they hold a soda in their hand and don't participate in those inappropriate activities. However, the outward innocence of the soda can may be overshadowed by the perception of some that because they are there, they approve of the immoral activities. That perception leads some to become targets of what others assume: that they would be willing to participate if invited. Further, the individual is at risk when peril presents itself because of their poor choice, and if they knowingly stay there, the Spirit may not be available to help in a moment of need. Even innocent intentions can lead to consequences that are serious for us and others. The Lord has pointedly counseled us on who we are to be and how we are to be perceived:

> Ye are the light of the world. A city that is set on an hill cannot be hid.
>
> Neither do men light a candle, and put it under a bushel, but on a candlestick; and it giveth light unto all that are in the house.
>
> Let your light so shine before men, that they may see your good works, and glorify your Father which is in heaven. (Matthew 5:14–16)

A light helps us and others to see clearly what is real, not what is perceived in the shadows. As lights to the world, we want others to see us clearly for what we are and what we represent. Our outward example must be coupled with an inward recognition of who we really are in the world and what is required of us. Think about the deeper meaning of the word *epistle* in the following scripture:

> Forasmuch as ye are manifestly declared to be the epistle of Christ ministered by us, written not with ink, but with the Spirit of the living God; not in tables of stone, but in fleshy tables of the heart. (2 Cor. 3:3)

An epistle is a writing that teaches or reveals something important to the reader. We as Latter-day Saints, along with all good religious people everywhere, have been called to serve as living epistles, to be an open-flame example of godliness. It requires us to go where

Christ would go, do what He would do, and live how He would live if He were in the world today.

I have wondered, if Christ openly walked the earth today, would He laugh and smile and have fun; would He have a sense of humor and recognize the humor in others? I believe He would, but it is such a refined sense of humor that would not in any way be at the expense of Himself, others, or the good name of His Church and work.

Don't get me wrong, the license plate is not sinful in any way, but it may bring frustrating consequences that flow from what seems to be an innocent and humorous way of thinking. It is a reminder of our responsibility to more carefully scrutinize the license plates we may innocently hang on our own lives.

Principle to Live By

Learn to avoid all appearance of evil or wrongdoing,
and we will avoid limiting consequences and
allow the Lord to bless us with further and greater
opportunities to influence others for good.

2

The Bird and Hubcaps

Focusing on what is real and avoiding reflections of the world

After high school, I went to play football for a small college in California. I was the only Latter-day-Saint, or Mormon, on the team, and everyone in school knew that. However, I did not attend institute but would park in the institute lot adjacent to the college because it was free. I parked as far away from the building as possible, so I did not have to talk to anyone about taking classes at institute.

On one occasion in that parking lot, I was taught a wonderful lesson concerning worldly preoccupations. At that time in my life, I had a puffy self-esteem and thought very highly of myself. I remember my grandfather once told me that there is always someone smarter, faster, better-looking, funnier, and so on, than I was. As he told me this, I thought to myself, *Yeah, right.* Unfortunately, that is where I was mentally and spiritually in my life. This context helps magnify the following experience.

As I mentioned, I thought I was too busy doing more important things than attending institute classes. I had unreasonable and unfounded aspirations to play at a major university and then maybe go on to the NFL. I was more interested in my image than school, work, church, or anything else. So, one day as I parked my car and headed for class, I heard a strange yet familiar sound echoing from my childhood, and I was taken back to a time when I would throw rocks or shoot a BB gun at empty tin cans. The hollow sound resonated in my ears and brought feelings that compelled me to search out where the sound was coming from.

As I walked around the parking lot, I finally discovered where the sound was coming from and found a small bird pecking at its own reflection in a chrome hubcap on a large van. I stood there watching this bird and noticed a silly pattern develop. The bird would forage along the blacktop near the van until it passed by a chrome wheel-guard, and upon seeing its reflection in the hubcap, it became distracted and would flutter in the air and peck away at the reflection until it was exhausted. The bird would then sit motionless on the ground with its feathers fluffed out until it regained its strength and then continue to forage. Incredibly, upon passing another hubcap, the bird again fluttered and pecked at its own reflection. I could not tell if the bird was trying to defend itself or was attracted to what it thought to be another bird. I was captivated by the bird's reaction to the reflection in the hubcap and its willingness to fall for the same distraction.

Finally, the bird flew away, and I stood there with a silly grin on my face, looking around to see if anyone else had witnessed the bizarre actions of this bird.

As I started to make my way across the street onto the campus, I thought to myself, *How did this bird not eventually realize that the reflection was not real after hitting the hubcap several times and knocking itself senseless?* You would think that this bird was intelligent enough to realize its actions were futile after several experiences with the hard object. Simply stated, how did this bird not learn the reflection was not real and its actions were futile?

As I walked to my class pondering the stupidity of this bird, something interesting and very personal happened. Out of nowhere, a very clear and distinct phrase came into my mind, "You are like this bird." I was so taken aback by this thought, thinking it was so not like me, that I did not immediately recognize it as a uniquely personal experience with the voice of the Spirit, the same Spirit I had been taught about since my youth but over time had become unresponsive to as a young adult.

After being taken aback by the thought that I could be like this silly little bird, my eyes of understanding were opened and the Spirit taught me it was true. What a shock to my youthful ego. I was going through life thinking I was just fine, busy doing some good things, at times even trying to develop myself in ways I thought were okay, but always having fantasies of grandeur in my mind's eye. I would see reflections of the world that were appealing to me and become sidetracked by those distractions. I felt normal, because it was what everyone I associated with did.

In the reflections that caught my attention, I saw myself with exotic cars, trendy clothes, high-paying jobs of prestige, positions of authority, expensive homes, jewelry that attracts attention, and wealth that commands respect. Like the bird, I would bounce off these reflections in my pursuit of the worldly goal, often becoming impatient and frustrated because they did not come to me as easily and quickly as I felt it did to others. I was only a young man, but I was so mentally locked in to those fantasies and expected them to happen by just wishing for them to occur and pursuing them aggressively. I figured it was just like athletics: you see it in your mind, and then you practice until it happens.

That day, the Spirit whispered to me these words, and I have remembered them as if they were spoken yesterday: "Winn, if you do not start focusing on what is real, you will be lost."

Who tells themselves that they are wrong and need to course correct or they will be lost? It had to be the Spirit chastising me, and it had such a profound impact on me that I turned around and enrolled in institute. You should have seen the looks on the faces of the institute staff and students who had been trying to get me to come for a long time. Everyone was shocked, but no more than I was.

Looking back with the long view, I can see that because of that experience I eventually went on a full-time mission, married in the temple, and changed my life forever. I have no doubt that experience was a tender mercy packaged in a teaching moment just for me. Does God really do that, package such personal teaching moments for each of us? I know He does, but we may often miss those moments if we are easily distracted by other things.

I have learned that what usually happens when in pursuit of worldly reflections is like what happened to the bird. We bounce off those reflections in an effort to grab hold of something that is not real until we are exhausted, devastated, and often spiritually broken. At times, some individuals are compelled to be humble, while the majority fall by the wayside and are lost in those false reflections that are not lasting. Brigham Young gave this sobering reminder to the saints in the Salt Lake Valley:

> Instead of reflecting upon and searching for hidden things of the greatest value to them, [the Latter-day Saints] rather wish to learn how to secure their way through this world as easily and as comfortably as possible. The reflections, what they are here for, who produced them, and where they are from, far too seldom enter their minds. (Discourses 7:282)

These are words of wisdom that extend themselves into our own experience today. There is certainly nothing wrong with having nice things, nor should we stop pursuing after a better life for our families and ourselves. After all, the riches of this earth are the Lord's to give, and there is a great deal of good that can be done with such resources. We should, however, not allow ourselves to become consumed with the pursuit. After all, we cannot take any of it with us when we leave this life. The Lord expressed Himself plainly when He warned:

> For where your treasure is, there will your heart be also.
>
> The light of the body is the eye: if therefore thine eye be single, thy whole body shall be full of light.
>
> But if thine eye be evil, thy whole body shall be full of darkness. If therefore the light that is in thee be darkness, how great is that darkness! (Matthew 6:21–23; see also 3 Nephi 13:21–23)

What we focus our eyes on and how we process it certainly determines what happens to our hearts. The Lord's words of caution were taught during His Sermon on the Mount, and again in our dispensation, the Lord has reiterated this counsel in the Doctrine and Covenants, stating:

> They seek not the Lord to establish his righteousness, but every man walketh in his own way, and after the image of his own God, whose image is in the likeness of the world, and whose substance is that of an idol, which waxeth old and shall perish in Babylon, even Babylon the great, which shall fall. (D&C 1:16)

More recently, in our day, the prophet Spencer W. Kimball observed:

> Modern idols or false Gods take the form of clothes, homes, businesses, machines, automobiles, pleasure boats, and numerous other material deflectors from the path of Godhood. What difference does it make that the item concerned is not shaped like an idol of stone? Brigham Young said . . . "I would as soon see a man worshipping a little God made of brass or wood as to see him worshipping his property." (*Miracle of Forgiveness*, 40–41)

We must learn to recognize the reflections of this world for what they are—deflectors from truth—and come to know what is real. So, what is real? Truth and light, which flows from God—that is real. If we learn to recognize the light and fix upon it for direction, we will not deviate so easily from it when those worldly reflections appear. Focusing on what is real is so important in this life, and discerning between worldly reflections and spiritual reality is the great challenge. Focus on Christ.

Principle to Live By

Learn to identify the reflections of the world for what they are and avoid them. Focus on Christ and His truth, and we will not be easily distracted, deceived, frustrated, or lost in pursuit of that which is temporary and unfulfilling.

3

ELEMENTS COMBINED

Being diligent in the things that matter

Most young boys like to throw things—anything. At least I did. Among other things, I remember throwing sand, dirt, water, and even striking matches and flinging them, all in fun, I would say. I loved westerns and watched every program that was on television, and it did not matter that most of them were in black and white—I just loved watching and imagining I was there. Even as a young boy I noticed there was a theme that developed in every episode: just before or during a fight between the bad guy and the good guy, a drink was thrown in the face of someone by the antagonist, or a cigarette was flung at someone to bait them into a scuffle, or during the fight someone always threw a handful of dirt in the face of a person to get an edge.

After every episode, I remember putting on my cowboy hat, my black high-top tennis shoes because they looked like boots, and going into the bathroom, locking the door, and spending forever in there practicing throwing water from a paper cup into my image in the mirror as if it were the face of my enemy. My poor mom probably could not imagine how that mirror was so water stained or why there was so much water pooled on the sink edge and counter. When I was outside playing by myself, I would practice throwing dirt in the face of my imaginary bad guy, which would give me the momentary edge I needed to get up and disarm him. Of course, I always won the imaginary fight.

I think I even tried it once on my brother when we were in a heated brotherly fight. I threw a cup of water in his face and then ran to lock myself in the bathroom. I remember as we got older getting into brotherly fights where I would have his head under my armpit in a headlock while raining blows on his head, when my mom would come in the room and tell me to stop it immediately and let him go.

As I matured, I realized this boyish playfulness was analogous to our spiritual lives. We can make the following comparison and then look at the inverse analogy. I call it "the elements combined":

- Dirt = obedience
- Water = scripture study
- Fire = prayer

It is interesting to consider the idea that if you were to take substances such as sandy clay, water, and heat, things I would fling around as a boy, they are, as individual elements in small amounts, not harmful to the life of an individual. But these elements can still cause minor irritation, frustration, and inconvenience when encountered in small amounts. However, if these elements are combined under the right circumstances and in requisite amounts, they can form an object that can be harmful and even deadly if thrown at an individual—namely a BRICK!

Now let's look at what happens by *not* doing things occasionally in small amounts that would seem to be no big deal. If we fail occasionally to study, pray, or be obedient, these occasional omissions may not be spiritually devastating. However, over time they do have a marked affect upon our attitudes and spirituality, and eventually our actions can become inappropriate. And most assuredly, if we combine these acts of omission regularly, they can ultimately be soul destructive.

We know as we exercise our faculties daily to study scripture, pray sincerely, and strive to be a little more obedient, we help ensure that our understanding is real, our lives remain focused, and we are blessed. Conversely, if we fail to practice these principles daily, we will start to see problems arise in our characters and attitudes, and we start to lay blame somewhere other than ourselves. Some even begin to blame God for their challenges.

In my own experience and in observation of others, it seems that an individual will hardly give any kind of meaningful service when they fail in their own lives to practice principles of progression. Learning to love, appreciate, value, and serve others will not happen as they need to for us and for others if we neglect those principles that bring the Spirit and foster a desire to look outside of ourselves.

Daily study of the scriptures, thoughtful communication with God, and following His commandments help insulate us from the evils of this world that are corrosive to the soul's inner chambers. Still further, such practices remind us of the Lord's curing process and the need for repentance daily, which will afford us the opportunity to change, be cleansed, and thereby receive the promised blessings of eternity. These are simple principles that have more than simple outcomes or results.

Alma, speaking to his son Helaman, addresses the idea that doing simple things, while foolish to some, is considered wisdom in the eyes of others:

> Now ye may suppose that this is foolishness in me; but behold I say unto you, that by small and simple things are great things brought to pass; and small means in many instances doth confound the wise.
>
> And the Lord God doth work by means to bring about his great and eternal purposes; and by very small means the Lord doth confound the wise and bringeth about the salvation of many souls. (Alma 37:6–7)

Simply said, it is doing the small and simple things daily that give value to monumental things required of us by the Lord. We further see this as the Lord tries to impress upon His servants how to deal with pressures that come from the world, and He expresses the need for attention to the small and simple things by using the example of a ship in a storm:

> You know, brethren, that a very large ship is benefited very much by a very small helm in the time of a storm, by being kept workways with the wind and the waves.
>
> Therefore, dearly beloved brethren, let us cheerfully do all things that lie in our power; and then may we stand still, with the utmost assurance, to see the salvation of God, and for his arm to be revealed. (D&C 123:16–17)

Likewise, we will find great strength and direction in the storms and pressures of our lives by being steady in doing the simple things daily that can have a profound influence in helping us cope with the challenges of life. The phrase "cheerfully do all things that lie in our power" is the key for me. To study, pray, and obey cheerfully is such a challenge at times, but it determines the quality of the experience.

On the other hand, a life devoid of such daily practices ensures we remain in our natural, lazy, and selfish existence, often useless to the work of the Lord in blessing humanity. President David O. McKay perceptively put it this way:

> Those who choose to remain in this material world and who close their eyes to the promise and possibility of a higher life, merely acknowledge that our purpose here is to be born, to live, breathe, prepare in a general way for those who follow after us, and then to die. (DNCS, *Deseret News*, The Church Section, June 8, 1935)

The thinking of the natural man is indeed narrow and limited. With the wonderful gift of intellect, and our moral agency, we find that the Lord has provided simple things that we can choose to do to bring about miraculous results for ourselves and for others.

Practicing principles of progression help us apply daily the balm that can cure us of the self-centered perspective of the natural man. Study, pray, and obey cheerfully every day.

Principle to Live By

Learning to be diligent in daily scripture study, prayer, and obedience to the Lord's commandments will help us deal with the pressures of life, increase our love for the Lord, ourselves, and others, and help us find purpose to our lives.

4

Olive Trees and a Boy's Punishment

The curing process of the natural man

My parents divorced when I was young, and when I was about seven, my mother remarried and we moved from a small modest home on the valley floor to a big beautiful home on a hillside. I thought we were rich! The home overlooked the city and had a distant ocean view. It was spectacular, especially at night or when the sun would gleam off the water. Because the home was elevated on a hill, we had a long curved and sloping driveway lined with about a dozen olive trees.

As young boys, my brother and I found that the olives were useful for only one thing—throwing or flinging around with slingshots. We would use olives we felt were the firmest because they could do the most damage. We would fire them at one another and throw them down into our neighbor's swimming pool.

As teenagers, we discovered we could take the olives and shoot them at one another with slingshots. What a discovery! We now could launch those babies farther and with greater power. We found that if we placed the odd-shaped fruit in the sling at just the right angle, it would curve around trees and boulders, making it impossible for our victims to hide from being pummeled during our childish neighborhood war games. My brother and I got so good at firing those fruit bullets with such accuracy that it became hard for us to find other kids willing to have neighborhood wars with us. This is important because our youthful wars using olives were a prelude to me coming to understand more fully the mortal conflict we find ourselves in and how we can come out victorious.

As I gained independence with age, those trees progressed from potential fun to outright punishment for my teenage transgressions. Over time, my parents quickly learned that hours of pruning the trees and sweeping up the fallen olives and leaves from the driveway was a more effective punishment than a spanking or writing. It was funny how my parents started with a spanking and then progressed to having us write some phrase that had something to do with whatever we did wrong one hundred to one thousand times, depending on the severity of the kid crime, to finally requiring legalized child slave labor to punish us and get some yard work done that no one wanted to do. It was brilliant, yet it was so frustrating for a young teenage boy because it took hours.

This kind of punishment was so time-consuming and painful that often I would beg for a quick crack of the belt or the cramping of my fingers in writing something I knew probably would not affect my behavior at all. My pleas went unheeded, so I learned to embrace that chore and began to learn about those trees. As strange as it sounds, those experiences later led me to a deeper understanding of the Atonement of Christ.

Over time, I learned that *Olea europaea* is the more romantic name for the European olive tree. Its ageless branches have been a symbol of peace, hope, and purity for centuries. The well-shaped fruit of the tree, the olive, is stingingly bitter to the palate in its natural state, until it has been cured. When the olive is pressed, soothing oil flows from it, carrying healing properties that are found in many of our medical ointments today. Godly wisdom has designated the pure oil of the olive for the spiritual and physical mending of the faithful. In the parable of the ten virgins in the Bible, oil is the key to preparation as the five unwise virgins ran out and had to go to purchase more. In the Lord's parabolic teaching to the Church concerning the ten virgins, notice what the oil represents in terms of preparedness:

> And at that day, when I shall come in my glory, shall the parable be fulfilled which I spake concerning the ten virgins.
>
> For they that are wise and have received the truth, and have taken the Holy Spirit for their guide, and have not been deceived—verily I say unto you, they shall not be hewn down and cast into the fire, but shall abide the day. (D&C 45:56–57; see also Matthew 25:1–13)

In the parable, the oil represents the Holy Spirit, and taking Him into our lives brings the guidance that we need to be prepared for the Lord's Second Coming. It is interesting then, that the restoring oil of the olive has long been symbolic of the Holy Ghost and the healing effect that the Spirit can have upon mortal man. It is the oil that fuels the lamp that is most significant; symbolizing how the spirit lights the soul to preparedness, giving spiritual vision out of darkness.

The meat of the olive, once pickled or seasoned, is very tasty and contains some nutritional value. Once cured, the olive becomes a welcome meal or garnish. Only the pit of the olive is discarded, as it is an obstacle and a distraction to the palate. Isn't it interesting that from a symbol of purity and gentility comes a fruit that is bitter and offensive until it has been cured of its natural state? Consider also the natural man, as King Benjamin gave sober attention to this thought:

> For the natural man is an enemy to God, and has been from the fall of Adam, and will be, forever and ever, unless he yields to the enticings of the Holy spirit, and putteth off the natural man and becometh a saint through the atonement of Christ the Lord, and becometh as a child, submissive, meek, humble, patient, full of love, willing to submit to all things the Lord seeth fit to inflict upon him, even as a child doth submit to his father. (Mosiah 3:19)

I love the comparison that from a divine source came fruit or offspring that through transgression became corruptible, bitter, and pitted with sin. It is here, in mortality that we learn to control the natural man and begin to cultivate characteristics of deity. Without the curing process of Christ's Atonement, we will remain in our natural state, bitter like the natural olive.

Fortunately, the curing process has been revealed and is available to everyone. The Lord has never given a commandment or exhortation for perfection without providing the process necessary for us to reach godly expectations.

This cure begins by giving attention to the Lord's direction through His spirit to redress the soul, "putting off the natural man" (Mosiah 3:19), as if removing the soiled garments of sin and weakness.

These soiled garments, once removed, call attention to the nakedness of man and his vulnerability to the weapons of the adversary. What we "put off" must be replaced with the garments of salvation, which serve as the armor of God. The Lord's invitation is sound:

> Wherefore, lift up your hearts and rejoice, and gird up your loins, and take upon you my whole armor, that ye may be able to withstand the evil day, having done all, that ye may be able to stand.
>
> Stand, therefore, having your loins girt about with truth, having on the breastplate of righteousness, and your feet shod with the preparation of the gospel of peace, which I have sent mine angels to commit unto you;
>
> Taking the shield of faith wherewith ye shall be able to quench all the fiery darts of the wicked;
>
> And take the helmet of salvation, and the sword of my Spirit, which I will pour out upon you, and my word which I reveal unto you, and be agreed as touching all things whatsoever ye ask of me, and be faithful until I come, and ye shall be caught up, that where I am ye shall be also. Amen. (D&C 27:15–18)

Putting on this godly armor helps to make the Lord's Atonement effective in our lives. It is impossible to be cleansed by the blood of Christ without acknowledging that we were a catalyst to the Lord's suffering in Gethsemane. It was suffering described as exquisite in nature because it was perfect and complete in its eternal application. Once our involvement is acknowledged, our understanding whispers that we not only seek forgiveness from the Father but from the Son also. To ask a friend to forgive us for the pain we have caused lubricates change and fosters humility that will facilitate the curing process. Once we have been dipped in the brine of painful remorse, those bitter feelings of guilt are drawn from our inner core like the poison from the bitter fruit. We then find the energy to help produce fruit from our own labors that are sustaining in nature and sweetened by the blessing of forgiveness. Learn of the Savior, and then learn from the Savior on how He can cure us.

Principle to Live By

Learn to embrace the curing process and power of the Atonement of Christ, be cleansed by His redeeming power, and enjoy the sweetness of His forgiveness.

5

The Commercial

Agency ensures consequences

The phrase "free agency" has always interested me because it is not found anywhere in scripture. It was Boyd K. Packer of the Quorum of the Twelve Apostles who taught the Church the doctrinal phrase that should be used when teaching about agency. The phrase is found in the Doctrine and Covenants:

> That every man may act in doctrine and principle pertaining to futurity, according to the moral agency which I have given unto him, that every man may be accountable for his own sins in the day of judgment. (D&C 101:78)

The phrase is "moral agency," which establishes that we have a moral responsibility to choose carefully, because there are consequences that follow our choices. Further clarity comes from another scripture in the Doctrine and Covenants:

> For behold, it is not meet that I should command in all things; for he that is compelled in all things, the same is a slothful and not a wise servant; wherefore he receiveth no reward.
>
> Verily I say, men should be anxiously engaged in a good cause, and do many things of their own free will, and bring to pass much righteousness. (D&C 58:26–27)

What is striking to me is that it says we are to use our agency to be involved in good causes. It does not say winning causes. Some may not join a good cause because they don't feel it is a winning ideal in today's world. But that is not the point; we are to do good things of our own free will and choice. After all, we are agents unto ourselves. As we talk about agency in terms of choices we make and the consequences that follow, I will share an experience I had with my son Dane.

Years ago, when Dane was a teenager, we sat down on a lazy Saturday afternoon and started to watch a movie. After some time, a commercial of a sensitive nature came on, advertising a product that promises to help control the outbreak of a specific sexually transmitted disease, so people could continue to be intimate. Kind of ironic when you think of it.

I absolutely hate commercials anyway, and to make it worse, it was a very uncomfortable subject, so my first inclination was to turn the channel. However, I felt impressed to watch it and see what kind of a reaction came from my son, who was at a dating age.

The commercial clearly stated that the product was only a treatment and not a cure. After the commercial, the movie resumed, and my son sat quietly watching and I thought to myself, *Okay, dodged that bullet.* After about five minutes, my son said, "Hey dad, remember that commercial that came on? What does that mean?" I just quickly said it was a product to help people with a personal problem. I felt so uneasy. He continued, "Yeah, but how do you get the disease?" I'm now thinking to myself, *Here we go. How am I going to explain this messy subject to my son?* I quickly, and a little flippantly, said something about how people who are promiscuous can pass on a condition that needs to be treated, although that is not always the case. He asked if there was any kind of a cure for such a condition, and I replied that there was no cure.

Now my son thought about it for a few more minutes, and then he asked if the only way you can get the disease is by being immoral. We talked briefly about how sometimes innocent people can be affected by the poor choices of others, and that not every person affected did something wrong. The conversation then shifted, and my son asked, "So if a person gets the disease by being immoral, can they repent and be forgiven?"

We then talked about how merciful and kind the Lord is and how when people make mistakes and then truly repent, the Lord will absolutely forgive them. Further, we talked about those who innocently are affected by the poor choices of others, and how they also need the healing aspect of the Lord's Atonement so they can deal with the emotional challenges that come with having the disease and being innocent. He was silent for a time and then asked something like, "So for a person who has made a mistake and is forgiven, can the Lord heal that person of the disease when they are forgiven? And why doesn't He heal the innocent person?" I told him that the Lord has all power to restore an individual physically, but for poor choices will not because it would destroy agency by diminishing or ignoring consequences and accountability for poor choices. For the innocent person, His Atonement heals in ways to help them deal with the emotional and psychological scars that they have to live with. Our conversation reminds me of the following verse that connects consequences to our choices:

> Wherefore, men are free according to the flesh; and all things are given them which are expedient unto man. And they are free to choose liberty and eternal life, through the great Mediator of all men, or to choose captivity and death, according to the captivity and power of the devil; for he seeketh that all men might be miserable like unto himself. (D&C 2:27)

It is true that we are free to make a choice, but we are not free to choose the consequences that follow. Further, when we have not made poor choices but are affected by the agency of others, we are agents unto ourselves to choose how we will respond when adversely affected in life. After a few moments of silence, he asked if a person who has the disease, repents, and is forgiven can be married in the temple. I am not sure why he was focused on the immoral aspect of this situation, and I did not care. I was getting excited because I believed he was making a connection. At this point, I thought I knew where he was going with his thought process. We talked about examples of the Lord's mercy and kindness in the scriptures and the power of His cleansing Atonement, and then he asked a question I did not see coming: "If a person makes a serious mistake, gets the disease, repents and is forgiven, and then goes to the temple to be married, do they need to tell the person they are going to marry that they have the disease?"

I asked him a question back: "What do you think would be the right thing to do?" He answered in an interesting way and said he believed that it would not be right to keep that a secret because you could give the disease to an innocent person. There was silence for a time, and I could tell there was more going on in his heart and his mind.

Finally, my son asked, "But what if you tell them you have the disease and they don't want to marry you?"

We both had long since forgotten about the movie and had a sweet experience discussing the potential challenges that flowed from such a confession. Christ clearly taught:

> Behold, he who has repented of his sins, the same is forgiven, and I, the Lord, remember them no more.
>
> By this ye may know if a man repenteth of his sins—behold, he will confess them and forsake them. (D&C 58:42–43)

There are a couple of things that need to be clarified here for our application of the doctrine of forgiveness. First, we confess serious sins to appointed priesthood leaders who hold keys as judges in Israel. We are not required in most instances to confess to others unless they have been affected by our actions. Secondly, when the Lord says He will remember those sins no more, we ought not to bring them up unless it is something that was so public and is widely known by others that we need to address it.

I have noticed in my career as a religious educator that, at times, individuals share things in class that they have struggled with, like pornography or how they are having trouble getting people to date them or in finding someone who has a desire to marry them because of their past. It certainly is a personal choice on how much to share with others about our past; however, if a person is still struggling with that kind of addiction or any other challenge, it may be important to share with a potential spouse your struggles and then allow them their agency to choose the direction they will take. The challenge then is dealing with a possible rejection.

The principle here is simply to be careful when making choices that can create future challenges for us. For my son, I think it was the first time he really began to grasp the connection between choices and consequences. He then said something that gave me confidence as he would soon begin dating; he promised me that he would never do anything morally wrong that could ruin his life or the life of another.

My son still had questions and concerns about the doctrine of repentance and forgiveness, but we had a moment together that was special and enlightening for both of us. That day, the commercial was so much better and important than the movie.

Principle to Live By

Learn to understand the connection between choice and consequence, and teach clearly and pointedly to others that when we choose wisely, we can avoid life-altering consequences for ourselves and others that can diminish our personal peace and happiness in this life.

6

SPAGHETTI AND THE MEXICAN WEDDING SHIRT

Stains can be removed,

but consequences may remain

Growing up in San Diego, California, we were influenced greatly by the Mexican culture since the border was not far away. We enjoyed the food, dress, music, and beautiful artwork found in Old Town San Diego. As a boy, I had traveled several times across the border into Tijuana. That is where I saw my first Mexican wedding shirt and fell in love with the design, and my desire to buy one stayed with me even after I got married.

My wife, Tina, worked for a time as a historical tour guide in Old Town, and it was fun to have her share the history of that unique place. On one of those visits to shop and eat, I bought a beautiful light-yellow Mexican wedding shirt with delicate embroidery on the front. I was so excited because of the memories I had as a young boy seeing those shirts in Tijuana. I loved how it fit loosely and had big pockets on the front with white hand stitching on the edges. It was my favorite shirt, and my wife and son often commented on how often I wore that shirt.

After wearing that shirt for years, I learned of its real value after an experience I had with my six-year-old son. Dane discovered he could bounce a ball off his tiny biceps and catch it in his hand—an important passage of coordination for most young boys. I remember as a boy practicing for hours until one day I was able to bounce and catch it every time. One evening at dinner, my son wanted to show me his newly developed skill. I have to admit, I wasn't really locked in to what he was trying to show me because I was distracted by the smell of dinner and a big plate of spaghetti sitting in front of me. I was starving!

Anyway, my son sidled up alongside me as I sat at the table looking at this plate full of spaghetti covered in red sauce and parmesan cheese. Before I realized what he was doing, my son popped the ball in the air and I caught sight out of the corner of my eye of something flying toward my food, and I caught it just over my plate. My reaction was just quick enough to avoid a mess, but my knuckles touched the sauce. Holding the ball in my hand, I gave the fatherly look to my son, handed the ball back to him, and pointedly said, "Do not do that again around the dinner table."

I'm sure you already know what happened next. As I was wiping off the sauce from my knuckles, my son backed away from the table and without hesitation popped it off his arm one more time. Unfortunately, I didn't see what he was doing until the ball landed in the middle of my plate, splattering sauce all over the front of my most favorite shirt.

I was so shocked that I got up without saying a word about my son's rebellious choice and lack of coordination. In quiet anger, I took off the shirt and started to throw it away, when my wife said she would spray it with stain remover and put it in the wash immediately.

My wife sprayed the shirt and then put it through the cycle, and amazingly the shirt indeed came out clean and fresh, and I was so excited! I put it on and it looked and felt great. So I hung it up and tempered my anger and frustration for my son's disobedience. All was well, I thought, and I would talk to my son later about what happened because I still had a plate of spaghetti to eat and I was starving!

A couple of days later I put the shirt on to wear outside on a family outing and looking down I noticed in the sunlight a faint outline where the shirt looked slightly discolored—it was exactly where the sauce had splattered. I was so disheartened and took the shirt off to hold it up in the direct sunlight to check it out more closely. In disgust I threw it in the trash. My wife rescued the shirt, and when I found it hanging up in the closet, I was irritated at first but let it go.

Interestingly, as I thought about that shirt over the coming days, I contemplated how the shirt was clean, fresh, and smelled good; it buttoned the same way and felt just as comfortable as before. However, the very faint outline of the stain in my mind changed how and when I would wear it. My wife said she could not see it, but I felt like I could see it, and more importantly, I knew it was there.

Not long after this experience, my son did something that we asked him not to do, and as I started to get upset with him, that shirt popped into my mind. It stopped me in my tracks, and it was a little dumbfounding to me, but I quickly realized I was being impressed upon by the Spirit not to do something rash out of anger that I would regret. I went to my closet, got the shirt, put it on, and the minute I walked into the room where my son was, he started to tear up and he said, "I'm sorry, Dad. I won't do that again." Amazing! I did not have to say a word; the shirt spoke loudly for me without me having to make a sound. That shirt was the best teaching tool I had ever used, and I was determined to keep it forever.

I learned that even though the shirt was clean and useful, I had to wear it differently from then on. From a spiritual perspective, being cleansed and having lasting consequences are mutually exclusive laws. I believe agency and consequences are analogous to this experience. Individuals may make poor choices, even seriously flawed choices that stain the soul for a time, and even though sincere repentance and change will apply the cleansing power of forgiveness through the Lord's Atonement, consequences may last a lifetime. In some cases, they may forever alter how one is used in the Lord's work.

Let me clarify. In no way am I trying to minimize the cleansing power of Christ's Atonement and His ability to restore and redeem even the vilest of individuals. There just needs to be a clearer connection by some between choice and consequence and the impact they can have on our lives.

Remember, my wife could not see the stain that I was sure was there. It can be a very real trial for some, after repenting and finding forgiveness to believe they have been forgiven and be able to forget the past and move on. There is an interesting example in scripture that I don't think stretches this thought too far:

> And ye shall offer for a sacrifice unto me a broken heart and a contrite spirit. And whoso cometh unto me with a broken heart and a contrite spirit, him will I baptize with fire and with the Holy Ghost, even as the Lamanites, because of their faith in me at the time of their conversion, were baptized with fire and with the Holy Ghost, and they knew it not.
>
> Behold, I have come unto the world to bring redemption unto the world, to save the world from sin.
>
> Therefore, whoso repenteth and cometh unto me as a little child, him will I receive, for of such is the kingdom of God. Behold, for such I have laid down my life, and have taken it up again; therefore repent, and come unto me ye ends of the earth, and be saved. (3 Nephi 9:20–22)

These verses deal with repentance and forgiveness and the invitation to come unto the Lord and be saved. For me a key phrase is "they knew it not." There may be times when people have accessed promised blessings because of their faith but do not immediately recognize them. Likewise, there are individuals who have been forgiven of their sins through sincere repentance and still may not know it because they are so focused on their mistakes and weaknesses in mortality.

Ultimately, even after having virtue restored and being cleansed by the Savior through our sincere repentance and His atoning blood, we may not see and feel the sweetness of forgiveness in our lives as we could, because of how we perceive ourselves. This requires us to be healed again by Christ's Atonement, in how we perceive ourselves. As much as we may need to be healed of sin itself, we may still need further healing mentally and emotionally as well. For some it may be a lifetime struggle, but Christ is merciful and patient with our weakness in mortality if we are willing to turn to Him.

This kind of mental and emotional healing can, in large measure, determine how we allow the Lord to use us. But regardless of past mistakes and poor choices in our lives, we can always find hope in Christ, be made clean, and be very useful in the Lord's work, if we allow Him to heal us for more than sin itself.

I have pondered this and what I have learned about the power of the Atonement of Christ simply because of a shirt. I am amazed at how we can learn profound things from very ordinary experiences in life. Finding lessons in our experiences helps mitigate the losses we may feel.

Principle to Live By

Understand that even though we can be cleansed and restored through Christ's Atonement, some consequences remain. When we falter, we can find hope in Christ, forgive ourselves, and move forward in life with a positive view of our own self-worth, knowing we still can be very useful to the Lord's work.

7

"Quakies" in the Snow

Looking and reaching upward

As we consider the importance of choosing wisely and consequences that flow from those choices, it is important to understand the purpose and outcomes of repentance and forgiveness.

In the mountains of Utah, above the town of Fairview, my stepfather built a circular cabin overlooking a large valley. His father was the first to build a cabin up in those mountains where he and his family would spend summers there among the beauty of the trees.

Over the years, my family and I have traveled up to the cabin most every summer to enjoy the beauty and serenity of the surroundings. Some of the most beautiful and amazing sights to me are the trees. The mountainsides are covered with them, and I love looking at them as we drive toward the cabin from the valley below.

In these mountains are some of the most colorful and beautiful trees on earth—the quaking aspen. Their shimmering leaves in the summer sun and the bright colors in the fall are a delight to look at. Over the years I have learned something very interesting that distinguishes this tree from all others. Aspens are grouped in families as they spread their roots underground in a familial root system. Therefore, you will see a forest of aspens with groups of different colors among one another. The bright yellow, orange, and red colors are hard to describe as they turn in the fall.

In the high elevations of Utah, winters are harsh on the small seedlings because the heavy snow causes some of the trees to bend over for most of the winter. As the snows recede, the sun beckons the trees again to strive to reach through the taller pines for their warmth and nourishment. This process reveals an interesting contrast among the trees. Many of the aspens grow tall and straight while others reveal twisted trunks. Some eventually grow straight and tall above the damaged part, while others cannot endure the heaviness of the snow and never find the height of the forest. Although the contrast is beautiful, we may be able to see a deeper beauty here as we draw a wonderful analogy from these aspens relating to the principle of repentance and forgiveness.

Our lives can parallel this beautiful and resilient tree: Many people grow tall and straight, reaching for the light of spirituality, surrounded by people who serve as examples and protectors to those tender in age and experience. All of us encounter challenges, trails, and afflictions that can scar and mark growth on our individual lives, and as with the aspen, these growth marks can enhance the beauty and value of a life when experience gives way to wisdom and its application.

In contrast, some among us struggle under the weight of challenges and sin and cannot seem to find the strength to push ever upward to overcome the weight of sin and its consequences. Still others find the resolve to push through, focusing on the nourishment offered from above, and ultimately straighten out and reach the same height of the other trees. Only a look downward reveals the scars and twisted trunks of these trees. Likewise, a look into the past reveals the scars of one's life, and if we dwell on those past mistakes, it can overcome our ability to focus on the Savior and His redeeming power that beckons us to look upward.

The Lord gave this important counsel for those coming out of the world:

> Go ye out from among the nations, even from Babylon, from the midst of wickedness, which is spiritual Babylon.
>
> But verily, thus saith the Lord, let not your flight be in haste, but let all things be prepared before you; and he that goeth, let him not look back lest sudden destruction shall come upon him.
>
> Hearken and hear, O ye inhabitants of the earth. Listen, ye elders of my church together, and hear the voice of the Lord; for he calleth upon all men, and he commandeth all men everywhere to repent. (D&C 133:14–16)

In the Lord's command for all to repent and flee the world of sin is this injunction to not look back. When people desire to change, it is the looking back in one's mind and heart upon those habits one has lived themselves into that can have such a draw upon us to cause us to return to those sins and lifestyle that lead to the destruction the Lord refers to. We must not look back but rather forward and upward to the Savior for His divine help, strength, and enabling power to lift us toward His light and spiritual nurturing until we grow above the twisted aspects of our past challenges.

Coupled with the Lord's counsel to not look back is the covenant we make each week as we partake of the sacrament to "always remember Him." When we become preoccupied with our past such that we are constantly reliving our behavior, then we have just offended the covenant by forgetting the Lord. To always remember Him means that we focus on His gifts and power to lift us and help us refocus our attention on His saving grace and redeeming power.

By way of reminder, past sins and mistakes need not be relived by looking back nor revealed to others after repentance and change have taken place. If the Lord will not dwell on our past misdeeds, then we ought not to continue to dwell upon them.

The great promise of the Lord that those sins will not be remembered carries with it the opportunity to be completely cleansed. The scriptures teach a clear and uplifting doctrine concerning repentance and forgiveness and the cleansing power of the Atonement. Paul taught the saints in Ephesus:

> Now therefore ye are no more strangers and foreigners, but fellow-citizens with the saints, and of the household of God. (Ephesians 2:19)

How does this happen, and what does it look like? I love the example found in the Book of Mormon about Alma the younger and the four sons of Mosiah:

> Now the sons of Mosiah were numbered among the unbelievers; and also one of the sons of Alma was numbered among them, he being called Alma, after his father; nevertheless, he became a very wicked and an idolatrous man. And he was a man of many words, and did speak much flattery to the people; therefore he led many of the people to do after the manner of his iniquities.
>
> And he became a great hinderment to the prosperity of the church of God; stealing away the hearts of the people; causing much dissension among the people; giving a chance for the enemy of God to exercise his power over them.
>
> And now it came to pass that while he was going about to destroy the church of God, for he did go about secretly with the sons of Mosiah seeking to destroy the church, and to lead astray the people of the Lord, contrary to the commandments of God, or even the king—
>
> And as I said unto you, as they were going about rebelling against God, behold, the angel of the Lord appeared unto them; and he descended as it were in a cloud; and he spake as it were with a voice of thunder, which caused the earth to shake upon which they stood. (Mosiah 27:8–11)

The horrible behavior of these young men who absolutely had been taught the truth by good parents constitutes open rebellion, something the Lord abhors because it can destroy the rights and freedoms of the whole society. Their behavior brings about an experience where an angel of the Lord gives them a compelling choice to repent or be cast off forever. In no way did this undermine their moral agency; but what could be more compelling than the command to repent or die? It was their choice.

In the next chapter we read something clarifying:

> And thus did the Spirit of the Lord work upon them, for they were the very vilest of sinners. And the Lord saw fit in his infinite mercy to spare them; nevertheless they suffered much anguish of soul because of their iniquities, suffering much and fearing that they should be cast off forever. (Mosiah 28:4)

Here they were described as the vilest of sinners, yet the Lord saw fit to reach out and save them and, more than this, to use them as instruments in His hands to save others. Here is the caveat to their experience: they did not have much success with those who saw their poor example. They ultimately found success with the Lamanites who did not know them. That was a consequence of their poor choices, and they were useful in a different way than they might have been among their own people. Continuing in the scriptures, we see the most beautiful part of this conversion story:

> Yea, verily, verily I say unto you, if all men had been, and were, and ever would be, like unto Moroni, behold, the very powers of hell would have been shaken forever; yea, the devil would never have power over the hearts of the children of men.
>
> Behold, he was a man like unto Ammon, the son of Mosiah, yea, and even the other sons of Mosiah, yea, and also Alma and his sons, for they were all men of God. (Alma 48:17–18)

We learn that some twenty years later, the general Moroni is in the middle of conflicts with Nephite apostates and the Lamanites who are their mortal enemies. Moroni is so good that the scriptures say if everyone were like him, then no evil would exist. The next verse is the most beautiful part of the description to me. Here, Moroni is now compared to the sons of Mosiah and to Alma and his sons, the same guys who were called the "vilest of sinners."

Think about the power of Christ's Atonement to take the vilest of sinners and make them as good as one of the greatest men to ever live. This means that no matter what an individual has done in the past, if he or she turns to Christ, He has the power to make that individual as good as the very best in life. His power to cleanse and redeem is beyond our ability to fully appreciate. Still further in Isaiah we find this great promise:

> Come now, and let us reason together, saith the Lord: though your sins be as scarlet, they shall be as white as snow; though they be red like crimson, they shall be as wool. (Isaiah 1:18)

What calming and cleansing knowledge flows from the Lord's atoning sacrifice for each one of us. Because of His redeeming power, we, like the aspens, can all continue to grow tall and straight above the challenges we sometimes face in our younger days.

Now is a good time for the caution. If we are not careful with some of our choices in life, even though we can be made clean, we may still be reminded of that sin for a lifetime by consequences that faintly remain in our minds and hearts. These outlined memories may keep individuals from receiving peace and finding service in the Lord's work because of a diminished self-esteem. And still further, if too serious, it may change how the Lord can use an individual to build up His kingdom. This in and of itself creates the continuing need for us and others to be touched and healed by the Savior's Atonement regarding how we think and feel about ourselves and others. We cannot minimize the consequences of poor choices, even though there is always hope in Christ's cleansing blood.

What powerful doctrine is taught in these verses concerning the cleansing and lifting power of the Atonement? The Lord's sacrifice and suffering not only can cleanse us of all iniquity, past and present, but it also has the power to lift and expand an individual to the highest plateaus of spirituality. This knowledge should motivate us to strive to make the Atonement of Christ effective in our lives by learning how to repent and believe we can be forgiven through the cleansing blood of Christ. Look upward to the light and not downward toward the darkness of the past.

Principle to Live By

If we learn to look upward to the light of the Savior, He can help us overcome any weakness and past mistakes to become spiritually straight and tall as are the aspens.

8

The Glass-Blowing Factory

Understanding the refining process and how to endure it

Opposition does not cause failure nor keep us from happiness. There are those who would excuse themselves from service and blame failure upon opposition that may exist within their lives. The fact is, there are many people who continue to find true happiness, joy, and great success in the very midst of this kind of opposition. The prophet Lehi tenderly taught his son Jacob concerning this principle of endurance:

> For it must needs be, that there is an opposition in all things. If not so, my firstborn in the wilderness, righteousness could not be brought to pass, neither wickedness, neither holiness nor misery, neither good nor bad. Wherefore, all things must needs be a compound in one; wherefore, if it should be one body it must needs remain as dead, having no life neither death, nor corruption nor incorruption, happiness nor misery, neither sense nor insensibility.
>
> Wherefore, it must needs have been created for a thing of naught; wherefore there would have been no purpose in the end of its creation. Wherefore, this thing must needs destroy the wisdom of God and his eternal purposes, and also the power, and the mercy, and the justice of God. (2 Nephi 2:11–12)

Opposition and persecution exist to test our integrity and provide opportunities to prove our allegiance to the Lord. Ponder for a moment the Lord's word:

> For he will give unto the faithful line upon line, precept upon precept; and I will try you and prove you herewith.
>
> And whoso layeth down his life in my cause, for my name's sake, shall find it again, even life eternal.
>
> Therefore, be not afraid of your enemies, for I have decreed in my heart, saith the Lord, that I will prove you in all things, whether you will abide in my covenant, even unto death, that you may be found worthy. (D&C 98:12–14)

Being willing to be divinely tested by the Lord is an important choice we make. Let me illustrate this point. One of my greatest memories was visiting a glass-blowing factory. Being artistically minded, I was intrigued with the process and loved to watch how they would make beautiful pieces of blown glass.

Workers would take large hunks of rock glass, mixed with other elements, and place them into large furnaces. These furnaces were heated to temperatures that would melt the glass until it was molten in form. This served to refine the glass by separating all impurities from it as they sunk to the bottom. The pure molten glass was then removed to another furnace, by buckets, from which artisans would draw the pliable material to work with. The artists would place a small piece on the end of a pipe, three to five feet long, and would gently blow into the pipe, shaping the glass.

Occasionally, the glass would need to be reheated in the furnace when it would begin to harden, and at other times the artist would roll the pliable piece of glass on an anvil to reshape it. Over time, the pliable glass material would take shape and become what the artist desired. Finally, the finished piece was put into a bucket of warm water to temper it. The end result was a beautiful piece of artwork that was useful and pleasing to the eye.

It was not until long after I had grown out of adolescence that I realized a similar process takes place in our lives daily. The Lord has said:

> Behold, I have created the smith that bloweth the coals in the fire, and that bringeth forth an instrument for his work. (3 Nephi 22:16)

When we remember that all things have been created and made to bear record of Christ, then even a process like this can be profound in helping us see the Savior and how He works in our lives. The following correlation describes the process:

- Rock glass = us
- Furnace = mortality
- Heat = opposition
- Melting = being humbled
- Artisan = the Lord
- Pipe = the gospel
- Blowing = the Spirit
- Pressing = chastisement
- Tempered = sanctification

This process was captivating for me. The Lord refines our souls in the furnaces of life through experiences, both good and bad. Gradually, the impurities of life are melted away, and over time we become pliable and teachable as we become sufficiently humble from such testing opportunities. I love another similar example of this process brought on by disobedience, but notice how the Lord characterizes those who will endure the Lord's refining process:

> I, the Lord, have suffered the affliction to come upon them, wherewith they have been afflicted, in consequence of their transgressions;
>
> Yet I will own them, and they shall be mine in that day when I shall come to make up my jewels.

> Therefore, they must needs be chastened and tried, even as Abraham, who was commanded to offer up his only son. (D&C 101:2–4)

Even good people can bring on challenges for themselves, and yet the process can still make them "jewels." It is interesting to me how a jewel is formed: heat, pressure, and time. These are things that we generally do not like to experience in our lives, let alone embrace them. But that is what is required to become precious to the Lord.

I love knowing that the Lord went through the same process even as a sinless individual. The scriptures teach this about Him:

> Though he were a Son, yet learned he obedience by the things which he suffered;
>
> And being made perfect, he became the author of eternal salvation unto all them that obey him. (Hebrews 5:8–9)

It is important to know and understand that the Lord had to go through the same process to become who He is. What is it about Christ that allowed Him to accept and endure this refining process? It is striking to me that of all the attributes and virtues that make up the character of Christ, the two He uses constantly to describe Himself are meekness and lowliness. This description is found in His invitation to come unto Him:

> Come unto me, all ye that labour and are heavy laden, and I will give you rest.
>
> Take my yoke upon you, and learn of me; for I am meek and lowly in heart: and ye shall find rest unto your souls.
>
> For my yoke is easy, and my burden is light. (Matthew 11:28–30)

In our dispensation the Lord has invited us to become like him in these words:

> Learn of me, and listen to my words; walk in the meekness of my Spirit, and you shall have peace in me. (D&C 19:23)

Meekness seems to precede all other virtues as it allows the Lord to shape us. Finally, by the Lord's gentle and indirect persuasion through the Spirit, our lives are cleansed and molded into instruments that are useful in the hands of the Master.

Ultimately, it is not opposition itself that helps us to develop character and strength, but rather how we respond once we have been acted upon by our situations in life. The important question becomes *How do we endure the refining process by responding appropriately?* Paul taught us well what it really means to endure when he testified:

> To them who by patient continuance in well doing seek for glory and honour and immortality, eternal life. (Romans 2:7)

To endure in the eyes of the Lord is to patiently continue doing good things even when it is not convenient or comfortable to do so. The principle of patience allows the Lord to manifest His power, goodness, and mercy in our lives—power that will refine us as instruments in His hands to bless the lives of others. Learning to embrace the refining process patiently makes us beautiful and useful.

Principle to Live By

If we learn to understand and endure the refining process, each of us can become a polished instrument in the hands of the Lord and serve to be a living example to those around us in seeing their potential through divine refinement.

9

The Donut and a Stick Shift

Responding to challenges appropriately

Years ago, I was taught a wonderful and humorous lesson concerning principles of endurance. I worked for a corporation that did not hold the same ideals of honesty that I espoused. I would travel several times a month to our corporate offices for meetings that consisted of negative feedback for my unwillingness to do things that were unethical. These trips caused me great anxiety, and I tried to distract myself from those uneasy feelings by stopping and buying donuts. I love all kinds of donuts, but my favorite is a plain cake donut.

On one of these trips, I made my usual stop at my favorite donut shop, called "Surfin Donuts," along the coast and bought two donuts: a plain cake and a plain old-fashioned along with some milk. Before getting back on the road I took a bite out of the plain cake donut. I had my donut in my hand, my milk in my lap, and another donut waiting in the sack—I felt better about my day!

As I started to merge onto the freeway, I had the donut in my right hand as I shifted into fifth gear. The movement for shifting into this gear is just a little bit different than the other gears because of the motion it requires. Suddenly, the donut flew from my hand over toward the passenger side door, bounced off the door, hit the dashboard, and finally landed on the passenger side floorboard, rolling to the far corner of the foothold.

My first reaction was to unbuckle and reach over to retrieve the donut, causing me to completely disappear from the view of what was ahead of me while barely keeping hold of the steering wheel. Suddenly I heard the rapid clicking sound of my tires running over the warning ruts on the shoulder of the freeway, and I quickly sat back up, realizing that wasn't the smartest thing to do.

As I thought about my situation, I saw that I had three options: (1) I could reach for the donut while in traffic, (2) I could forget about that donut and eat the one I had left in the bag, or (3) I could pull over where it was safe, retrieve my lost donut, assess the damage, and decide what to do.

The funny yet ludicrous thing is, I thought about those three options for ten minutes before deciding to pull over, check out my donut and decide whether it was still good for eating. I found the donut to be in good shape and edible, so I finished both donuts, washing them down with my milk, and then hit the road.

As I thought about that strange and funny experience while finishing my trip to the office, I realized there was a correlation to our lives. When bad things happen to us, we have choices to make. In this instance, the Lord did not cause the donut to fly into the corner floorboard, and I did not throw it there; it just happened. Regardless of the cause, when bad things happen, we can either (1) do something stupid and dangerous to our own spiritual welfare, (2) lose faith completely by giving up and turn our attention to something else to try and appease ourselves, or (3) patiently think through what is happening, assess the situation, and then act in wisdom under the influence of the spirit. The last option is the hardest to trust because it requires time and can cause us some inconvenience when we feel like responding immediately.

As I pondered this, my mind caught hold of an impression that I would need to "remember the donut" when I got to the corporate offices. My anxiety quickly returned.

Sure enough, the meeting went just as I feared: horribly. I was threatened with losing my job unless I would compromise my integrity for the sake of corporate profits. As I started to get angry, the image of that donut popped into my mind and I could see it perfectly. I wasn't even listening to the person yelling at me but was thinking about my three potential responses. (1) I could reach across the desk and strangle this guy—who in my mind deserved it, (2) I could resign and look for another job, leaving my family in a pinch financially, or (3) I could be patient and return home to assess my situation and make a wise decision using inspiration. Fortunately, I chose the third.

On my drive home, I was somewhat grateful for the spiritual heads up. A few days later, I was terminated without notice. I turned to the scriptures. As I was reading and wondering how I was going to support a family and a mortgage, I came across my answer in a couple of passages that I had not understood before. Notice the doctrine of how God delivers us:

> I would that ye should do as I have done, in remembering the captivity of our fathers; for they were in bondage, and none could deliver them except it was the God of Abraham, and the God of Isaac, and the God of Jacob; and he surely did deliver them in their afflictions.
>
> And now, O my son Helaman, behold, thou art in thy youth, and therefore, I beseech of thee that thou wilt hear my words and learn of me; for I do know that whosoever shall put their trust in God shall be supported in their trials, and their troubles, and their afflictions, and shall be lifted up at the last day. . . .
>
> And I have been supported under trials and troubles of every kind, yea, and in all manner of afflictions; yea, God has delivered me from prison, and from bonds, and from death; yea, and I do put my trust in him, and he will still deliver me. (Alma 36:2–3, 27)

It became clear to me that God generally delivers us *in* our afflictions while we are most often looking to be delivered *from* our afflictions, a subtle but profound difference in the doctrine of deliverance. If I am always looking and praying to be delivered *from* those trying times, then I will become even more discouraged when each day passes and freedom has not come. But if I understand that I am delivered *in* my darkness, then I will be focused on identifying each day how I was blessed to help me through the trouble hounding me. My love for God and Christ, and gratitude expressed by what I choose to focus on while I am in my daily struggles, is key. But I still needed to learn more, and it came in another passage. Notice here the three principles that will help us endure.

> Verily I say unto you my friends, fear not, let your hearts be comforted; yea, rejoice evermore, and in everything give thanks;
>
> Waiting patiently on the Lord, for your prayers have entered into the ears of the Lord of Sabaoth, and are recorded with this seal and testament—the Lord hath sworn and decreed that they shall be granted.
>
> Therefore, he giveth this promise unto you, with an immutable covenant that they shall be fulfilled; and all things wherewith you have been afflicted shall work together for your good, and to my name's glory, saith the Lord. (D&C 98:1–3)

Coupled with the doctrine of deliverance are principles we must practice that give life to the doctrine. We must strive to be patient, cheerful, and faithful during the hard times we encounter in life. I could see how these three character-building principles could help me endure this trial, but I did not think it was fair that I should have to endure them when I was trying to be honest and worthy in the first place.

That attitude reminds me of a time in my life when I was a teenager trying to improve myself and some challenges came up. I said within earshot of my dad something like, "It's not worth trying to be worthy. Every time I try to be better something bad happens." My dad just calmly said, "Yes, you can look at it that way, or you can be happy because you are worthy to receive the help you need to get through these things." He was right, and I knew it. The fact is that challenges, trials, and afflictions come to all people, believers or not. In those moments, it is nice to know that because we are striving to be worthy, we are entitled to the Lord's help to deal with the unwanted experiences of life.

Ultimately, we need to be willing to learn to be more patient and receive the help we so desperately need, and find happiness in our experiences here.

Principle to Live By

When we are willing to be more patient, cheerful, and faithful during our difficult challenges in life, we can find joy in the knowledge that we are entitled to the Lord's help, and we will be looking for that daily deliverance and have a desire to express our gratitude for it.

10

The Old Widow and the Charlie Brown Christmas Tree

Serving others silently

I remember having some interesting Christmas experiences when I was young. There was a time when money was scarce, so we collected tumbleweeds and put them on top of one another and painted them green to look like a tree. Try hanging ornaments on a tumbleweed!

Because I love Christmas so much, this was a perfect time for me to learn my first lesson in quiet giving, which came long before I read of the Lord's frequent acts of quiet service. At an early age, I remember my wonderful mother often giving aid, openly and silently, to others in need. My first opportunity to participate came while I was still a young boy, when my mother suggested that we help brighten the life of another person by doing a kindly deed. My mother was a single parent raising three small children and we were struggling financially, but she gently and persuasively led us to choose a woman named Olive Short. What a perfect choice; Olive was a poor elderly widow woman in ill health. My mother took me, my brother, and sister to the store to buy a small Christmas tree, ornaments, and some lights to make it sparkle, along with a few small gifts.

My mother allowed us to choose the tree, and it didn't matter that the tree was short and sparsely pined—very reminiscent of the little tree Charlie Brown picked out in the classic program I still watch every Christmas. The important thing was that our choice was sincere. We took our gifts to Olive's home after dark so as not to be seen. Of course, as children we wanted to stay and see Olive's reaction and experience her expression of gratitude; after all, she might have something for us in return. My dear, wise mother explained that this gift of love needed no name or reciprocation. We would give quietly and in secret.

As we pulled up to her block, we were instructed carefully on where to place the gift, when to ring the doorbell, and how to return to the car without being seen. Youthful feet and energy proved quicker than the shuffle of the widow's walk, and we easily made it back to the car undetected. As Olive opened the door, we watched for a moment and then slowly drove away. Although it was dark and the distance far, I was still able to see and shall ever remember her surprised look as she cupped her face in her feeble little hands. Even at a tender age, I knew her expression was one of complete joy because she knew someone cared.

Our drive home was a silent one. I didn't know what the others were thinking, but I'm sure it was like what I felt inside: a sense of warmth that told me we had done something simple and yet so wonderful—something for nothing in return. My quiet contemplation was pierced with a silent and yet penetrating voice within my mind that whispered, *Thank you.*

I watched my mother closely that night as we drove home, perhaps more closely than ever before, and thought to myself how lucky we were to have her as a mother to teach us a better way of life.

The years have come and gone since that experience, and yet deeper lessons have been learned concerning how we can serve others.

The Lord's mortal sojourn is the greatest example of a life dedicated to lifting others to higher plateaus of spirituality through service. Scriptures testify that it was Christ who took the man Saul, a persecutor of godly people, and brought forth Paul the proselyte. Matthew, a despised collector of taxes, became a renowned gatherer of knowledge; and Peter, who was impetuous and emotional, became spiritually solid and reliable. Then there was Mary of Magdala, a virtuous woman who found favor in being the first to see and hear the risen Lord. And in our dispensation, He took a common farm boy who was a feller of trees and a sower of seed and brought forth Joseph, a prophet of God and restorer of truth. The Lord did this quietly and individually over time. And when He did do things openly, He asked people to not noise it abroad. Consider this example:

> When he was come down from the mountain, great multitudes followed him.
>
> And, behold, there came a leper and worshipped him, saying, Lord, if thou wilt, thou canst make me clean.
>
> And Jesus put forth his hand, and touched him, saying, I will; be thou clean. And immediately his leprosy was cleansed.
>
> And Jesus saith unto him, See thou tell no man; but go thy way, shew thyself to the priest, and offer the gift that Moses commanded, for a testimony unto them. (Matt. 8:1–4)

There are certainly other gospel meanings of why the Lord asked this man to tell no one within the context of what is going on at this time in the Lord's ministry, but it does magnify the Lord's desire to serve without fanfare. Sometimes, attention diminishes the service rendered and can create another set of challenges. Still, quiet service can have results that are openly seen by others and praised for its outcomes.

It is certain that in our own lives, our support and influence will not be as dramatic or as visible as was the Lord's. Yet, it is just as important to His work and our own personal salvation. The late Edwin Arlington Robinson, distinguished American poet, once wrote of gratitude:

> Two kinds of gratitude: The sudden kind we feel for what we take, and the larger kind we feel for what we give.

To most of us, this first kind of gratitude is more familiar. It is the pleasure and warmth we feel when something is given to us to make us feel acknowledged and loved, and what a great feeling this is. However, too often our kindness is prompted by us receiving a gift first, and the prompting feelings that flow from the gift offered causes us to act in kind. The second gratitude, while very rare, is simply more wonderful and real. How special we feel when we have taken the time and opportunity to brighten and lift the life of another for no other reason than out of love. We feel deeply grateful for the opportunity to show our goodwill and sense of Christian charity, while expressing our love for God. As a result, this second kind of gratitude and Christian service is often best expressed through quiet acts of love and concern. Do something good and don't get caught.

Principle to Live By

If we learn to be of service to others quietly and silently, we will be emulating the Savior's life of service and bless the lives of others in ways yet unseen. And the Lord will reward us with the warmth of His Spirit to the filling of our souls.

11

New Basketball Shoes and the Homeless Man

Serving others openly without expectation

My wife's parents were divorced after she graduated from high school, and her father lived alone in a small place with very few people to associate with. It was a tradition for my wife's family each Christmas holiday to go to Balboa Park in downtown San Diego to look at the Christmas lights, and so we continued that tradition for her dad. One holiday, I had received a pair of basketball shoes for my birthday in early December from my mother. This is not unusual, except that they were rather expensive shoes and not the kind we could afford as a young married couple, and they were greatly appreciated.

On the night we planned to go downtown, I was wearing my new basketball shoes and it was a cold and drizzly night. After picking up my father-in-law, I noticed a man walking on the sidewalk with no shoes or socks, tattered pants, and a torn T-shirt petitioning people for help. It was obvious he was being rejected at every turn, and as I watched this man being rejected time and time again, I petitioned Heavenly Father silently in my heart for someone to help that man. The thought came into my mind, *You help him.* I quickly passed off the thought as I drove beyond him and was not in position to do so. Again, I petitioned the Lord to help him and the thought quickly returned, *You help him.* I thought to myself, *How in the world can I help this guy?*

I decided to backtrack several blocks so that we would drive toward the man again. As I saw the man in the distance, I wondered what I could possibly do to help him; I had no cash, no food, and no clothes to give. Suddenly the thought came, *Give him your shoes.* I flinched, not so much because they were an expensive gift to me, but because I did not want to make anyone uncomfortable in the car having an unusual exchange with a homeless person and the fact that I would be driving without shoes. By now I was upon the man and my moment came to either act or ignore.

As I pulled over, I asked my wife to roll down her window, and she did so with a questioning look on her face. I called to the man, and as he approached the car, I removed my shoes and handed them to him through the window. I sat there with anticipation, waiting for a thank you or an invoked blessing for my gift, but the man matter-of-factly responded, "Don't you got any socks with these things?"

This was not the response I expected. I was shocked, and with some indignation I removed my socks and handed them to my wife to give to the man through the window. Without a word, the man turned and walked to an overhang, sat down, and put on his new socks and shoes.

I slowly drove away feeling humiliation and anger for my stupidity in helping someone who lacked appreciation for my sacrifice. As I drove away, I glanced over to my wife and could see the emotion on her face. I felt somewhat relieved and less ashamed by her tenderhearted response, and as I thought more about the exchange, my anger softened.

Further thought on what just happened validated the man's response. After all, he was cold, hungry, tired, and rejected at every turn; why would he be thinking about anything other than survival? This reminds me of an experience the Lord had with a group of lepers:

> And as he entered into a certain village, there met him ten men that were lepers, which stood afar off:
>
> And they lifted up their voices, and said, Jesus, Master, have mercy on us.
>
> And when he saw them, he said unto them, Go shew yourselves unto the priests. And it came to pass, that, as they went, they were cleansed.
>
> And one of them, when he saw that he was healed, turned back, and with a loud voice glorified God,
>
> And fell down on his face at his feet, giving him thanks: and he was a Samaritan.
>
> And Jesus answering said, Were there not ten cleansed? but where are the nine?
>
> There are not found that returned to give glory to God, save this stranger.
>
> And he said unto him, Arise, go thy way: thy faith hath made thee whole. (Luke 17:12–19)

Here is why I use this example: I don't believe the Lord had an expectation that any one of the lepers would return to thank Him; He did it because they had a need and petitioned Him for help. However, when the one returned to praise Him, it was natural for the Lord to ask where the others were. Then the Lord quickly focused on the man's faith and sent him on his way.

In my example, all that mattered was that there was a need, and although the homeless man was not petitioning me directly, I saw it and it became a petition to me when the Spirit whispered to help him. After all, I asked the Lord to help him. If I were more like the Lord in that moment, I would not have expected a certain response. There was a need, and I met it the best I could under the circumstances, and that was all that mattered. It is not even relevant that that man would probably be robbed of those shoes by others on the street who would notice them; I was still obligated to follow the answer to my petition for that man's need.

I learned a valuable lesson that night concerning my service to others. Whatever my offering to others, it must be done without expectation, and because I had anticipated a specific, even self-indulgent response, I was blindsided by those expectations, which undermined my motive for serving in the first place. I had to ask myself if I was really trying to help a child of God out of compassion, or if I was soliciting a feel-good response to feed my warped sense of Christian charity. I failed in my attempt to serve another that night, although I did help fill a basic need for that man. Ultimately, I was the one best served with a deeper understanding of the need to serve without expectation.

Principle to Live By

If we learn to be of service to others, silently and openly, without expectation, the Lord will silently and openly bless our lives.

12

Chocolate and a Covenant

Being involved in the rescue

An exemplary life may be measured by one's willingness to give of themselves to others, openly and silently, without personal expectation. The *straight* and narrow path of direction always leads to the *strait* and narrow path of saving conduct. Likewise, before we can express a pure love and concern for the spiritual welfare of our fellow man, we must first experience and understand in small measure the Lord's charity for us as individuals and Heavenly Father's love for His Son. My experience came through my own son one summer afternoon. Let me start with some context.

Shortly after I returned home from my mission, I met my beautiful wife, and one year later we were sealed in the Los Angeles Temple. In that holy place, we received the promises and blessings of posterity given to Abraham, Isaac, and Jacob, blessings spoken of in our patriarchal blessings. We held on to those promises that we would have children in this life and watch them grow to manhood and womanhood and be stalwart members of the Church.

We entered our marriage with a great deal of excitement and anticipation for what the near future would bring. Subsequently, we struggled for the next seven years to conceive, losing multiple pregnancies to miscarriage. As we pondered adoption, we felt impressed to approach Heavenly Father with our desires to have children. What followed was that Heavenly Father extended an invitation for us to enter into a covenant with Him to realize our righteous desires. We then made certain promises to improve our lives spiritually and offered up a sacrifice of chocolate as part of a six-month covenant. Why chocolate? Because we ate it every day and that would remind us of our covenant. As silly as that may sound to some, the principle of truth in relation to sacrifice is that unless the Lord specifically identifies the object of sacrifice, he cares only that it is important to us at the time; otherwise it is not a sacrifice at all. And since we enjoyed chocolate daily, this would certainly remind us daily of our sacred promises.

As we entered this covenant period, we felt impressed that our faith would be tested, and we vowed to be faithful to the end under all obstacles without murmur or complaint. This became increasingly difficult as each month passed without consequence. The natural man wants it now, and I certainly did. Yet we remained faithful to the end and true to our promises, even though we discovered at the end of the sixth month Tina was not pregnant. As we reflected upon the experience, we felt a desire to continue the covenant for one more month as a sign of our faith and love for Heavenly Father and the Lord. It was our way of showing we would remain faithful even if for some reason our desire was not realized.

At the close of the seventh month we discovered that my wife was pregnant. The doctor, unaware of our situation, calculated the possible time of conception to be the final days of the sixth month. The Lord had kept his promise as we had kept ours.

Nine months later, my wife gave birth to a healthy boy. The Lord had given us a son. Because of the circumstances surrounding our son's birth, we have some very tender feelings for him as our only son. As a father, I have a deep appreciation for having a son to pass on my family name and priesthood promises. I share these very personal things so that you may understand more fully the experience I am about to share.

When my son was three years old, my grandparents came to California from Utah for a visit. Being lovers of the ocean, we decided to take them across the ferry to a resort island to shop and take pictures. After a time, my wife asked me if I would watch Dane while she went shopping with my grandmother. At the time, my grandfather was taking pictures from the ferry landing of the city skyline across the bay. Being a lover of art, I soon decided that I wanted to visit a nearby gallery, and feeling that a three-year-old boy would not be appreciated in a prestigious gallery full of expensive artwork, I called out from a distance to my grandfather and asked him to watch Dane for a few minutes. He turned and waved as he smiled, and then I was off.

After a time, I returned to the pier at the same time my wife and grandmother arrived, and my wife asked me where Dane was. I told her Grandpa had been watching him and asked him where he was. My heart sank as Grandpa responded that he didn't know, and he was unaware that I asked him to watch our son. It was my fault, and I knew it. I assumed Grandpa understood me, when in reality he thought I was just waving to him on the pier.

We quickly looked around but saw no sign of our son. We anxiously checked the ferry boat to see if he had climbed back on board, but when we did not find him there, panic set in as we thought perhaps he had fallen off the pier into the water. We frantically searched the pier and waterfront and silently prayed for the welfare of our son. Our search now expanded to the surrounding shops without success, and then absolute horror filled my soul as I believed he may have been abducted. I cannot adequately express the feelings of despair that clouded my mind and heart with the idea that we had lost our son—our only child.

Suddenly, a young mother walked out of a shop in the distance holding her son's hand, and clinging to her little boy's hand was my son. This mother must have recognized the panic expressed on our faces because she called out to my wife. At the very moment my gaze fixed upon my little boy, I felt an uncontrollable sense of joy, relief, and gratitude for his safe return. As we embraced, I had a feeling of love so exquisite that it transcended everything I had experienced before.

This experience gave me a special appreciation for the love our Heavenly Father has for His Son and a greater understanding for the sacred reunion we may all enjoy one day. I have pondered in reverence what it must have been like for Heavenly Father to fix His gaze upon His Son and embrace Him as He returned triumphant and safe. What a feeling of joy must have filled the Father's bosom, and what expressions of love They must have exchanged as They embraced. I have thought about what it might be like for us to experience this same kind of reunion, as Heavenly Father and the Lord embrace us tenderly upon our triumphant and safe return home, and, still further, the reunion with loved ones who have gone before us.

Further thought has led me to reflect upon our Heavenly Father's children who are lost or in search of the truth, and the sacred duty to slow down, reach out, and minister unto them. To help them comprehend this promised heavenly reunion, the Lord expressed it this way:

> Remember the worth of souls is great in the sight of God;
>
> And if it so be that you should labor all your days in crying repentance unto this people, and bring, save it be one soul unto me, how great shall be your joy with him in the kingdom of my Father!
>
> And now, if your joy will be great with one soul that you have brought unto me into the kingdom of my Father, how great will be your joy if you should bring many souls unto me! (D&C 18:10, 15–16)

Certainly, our most important convert is ourselves, then our loved ones and friends, and finally our fellow men. To think upon the feelings of joy, gratitude, and love that will flow in loftier spheres stirs the soul to greater desires of service to God and our fellow men. We can help find, and return safely home, sons and daughters of a loving Father and Mother in Heaven.

I think too often we get caught up in the fast pace of life and forget that we have been called to minister unto people and not programs. A wise friend once taught me that we must not get caught up in the trappings of our titles and callings so much that we forget we have been called to the ministry. We should be off to the rescue of one another, member and non-member, active and less-active—everyone needs to be found. Prepare for heavenly reunions by helping others find safety in mortality.

Principle to Live By

If we truly learn to minister to one another in the Lord's way, we will find salvation for ourselves as well as for others, and we can look forward to an indescribable reunion with those we love and those who love us.

13

"Fat of the Land"

Sinking roots deep in the gospel of Christ

Coming from good pioneer stock, I have been taught somewhat concerning the "fat of the land." My grandparents were raised in Utah and had a deep appreciation and understanding of the principles of sowing and reaping.

I am grateful for what they taught this city dweller concerning sowing and reaping and how these principles parallel life as a Latter-day Saint. This knowledge has enhanced my appreciation for all things green, growing, and colorful; I love looking at beautiful landscapes, gardens, trees, shrubs, and so much more when I am outside. That's just how I roll, and I know so many others feel the same way. In fact, one of the greatest signs of spirituality is a love for nature.

So what have I learned from the wisdom of others and the appreciation for all things natural? I have learned that when a fruit seedling is planted, certain steps must be followed to ensure the strength of the tree and its future harvest. The tree not only needs good soil, sun, and water, but it also requires wise use of these elements. For instance, it is unwise to use too much water in the beginning because it may weaken the roots—the roots do not have to work to supply water to the limbs by stretching deep into the earth, and as a result they will remain close to the surface, where they may easily weaken and dry with the heat. However, if the tree for a time is watered lightly and allowed to develop, it will cause the roots to reach deep into the soil in search of nourishment. The tree needs help in the nourishing process and the opportunity to self-develop as much as possible, so we train it and allow it to work for its own nourishment.

Deep roots are strong and secure because they have worked themselves into a position where they are not easily dried or weakened by drought. This is critical, for if the roots are not sufficiently strong, the branches may outgrow the roots, which will eventually cause the tree to wither and die or bear bitter fruit. This occurs because the branches take strength unto themselves to survive.

A similar process takes place spiritually in the church today. The youth of Zion, like the seedling, start out with the potential to bear fruit that is nourishing. All the elements for nourishment are available; however, much like the seedling, they too must be applied wisely and early so that the roots of faith may be sustaining in nature. The roots should nourish the branches and not vice versa. Likewise, our testimonies should nourish and sustain the individual and not the organization. The Church is only here to help individuals and families live the gospel of Jesus Christ. The gospel itself is nourishment. Ultimately, strong testimonies strengthen the Church.

Jacob, the younger brother of Nephi, understood this principle. In his writings, Jacob teaches the allegory of the olive tree. Notice his observation:

> Have not the branches thereof overcome the roots which are good? And because the branches have overcome the roots thereof, behold they grew faster than the strength of the roots, taking strength unto themselves. (Jacob 5:48)

This has application today as the Church has become a strong organization unto itself through the direction of the Lord's chosen vessels and the combined efforts of the Saints. However, the individual has not always drawn strength in concert with the Lord's organization. That is our personal responsibility. The Church has provided programs for our youth; however, at times in the past we may have catered too much to the entertainment of the youth of Zion, much like over watering the seedling. Individuals may be entertained but not necessarily sufficiently strong enough to endure the focused heat of the adversary. Conversely, some parents have tried to shift the burden of teaching their children upon the Church, thus forsaking the Lord's counsel:

> And again, inasmuch as parents have children in Zion, or in any of her stakes which are organized, that teach them not to understand the doctrine of repentance, faith in Christ the Son of the living God, and of baptism and the gift of the Holy Ghost by the laying on of the hands, when eight years old, the sin be upon the heads of the parents.
>
> For this shall be a law unto the inhabitants of Zion, or in any of her stakes which are organized.
>
> And their children shall be baptized for the remission of their sins when eight years old, and receive the laying on of the hands.
>
> And they shall also teach their children to pray, and to walk uprightly before the Lord. (D&C 68:25–28)

When we shift our divinely mandated responsibility to others, the result is that many of our youth have taken strength unto themselves from the world, overcoming the roots of faith. If our roots are not sunk deep in gospel sod, our branches may not draw strength to give shade to our youth who are tender and underdeveloped in testimony. Without strong testimonies, the fruit of conversion cannot come to harvest.

Strong roots come from nurturing hands. Youth will learn best from our daily examples of faithful service where we stand, which is evidence of our own testimonies. Our young people must hear the gospel in its purity when possible in our homes, then see it in action, experience it, feel the workings of the Spirit, and learn to crave it for themselves. The announcement in the October 2018 general conference of the new gospel home study curriculum that will be supported at church will certainly help with this important spiritual priority—if implemented in our homes.

Principle to Live By

If we sink our roots of faith deep in gospel soil, we will not be overcome by the heat of opposition, and we will not only produce good fruit from our labors, but also help others tender in testimony to be planted firmly in the gospel and become a strength to the Lord's church and His work.

14

A Toss of the Coin

Self-mastery brings a life of quality over quantity

When I was in the business world, I had a couple of partners in a marketing business where we would create marketing plans for professionals.

A popular marketing technique in today's fast pace of commercialism is the sale. The sale of a product, service, or person. Who doesn't like a good sale?

For me, the idea that I am getting more for less feels important—so I can continue to buy more for less. It is an endless mindless cycle if you think about it. If we continue to buy more for less, ultimately aren't we just spending more?

This kind of thinking is evident in the lives of many individuals today who strive to surround themselves with as much as possible to appease unfulfilled emotions, passions, and appetites. Because they are not satisfied, they constantly seek more for less to fill the many voids that exist in their lives. This kind of attitude is a direct result of a lack of self-control.

Our society has become obsessed with quantity, goods, money, or even added years. A pursuit of material things becomes all an individual has when the reservoir of spirituality is dry.

It is self-control that brings a quality to life and helps us avoid the search for excess. It brings quality because of what we become by it, not for what we do or receive. Emotions, passions, and appetites are fulfilled appropriately, in ways that allow us to maintain our dignity and honor. There exists a proper balance to life because there is control, and not slavery to things of this world. Self-respect comes from *striving for the mastery.*

This search for quantity reminds me of a story I once read about a rare coin that had been discovered and bore a contrasting inscription. One side read "quantity," the other "quality." Although little is known of the coin's origin, or even its intended message, it suggests a real dilemma of epic proportions faced by every age. Do we focus on quantity or quality in our own lives?

A scriptural comparison is appropriate here. Methuselah, whose life may have paralleled the making of this coin, could well represent a life of quantity. Many people today would desire to live a life as long as his. Biblical accounts reveal Methuselah lived 969 years, perhaps the longest-lived person ever. Certainly, this is a quantity of years that would suggest a life full of accomplishment. Imagine how he must have developed his talents, and the many acts of service he must have rendered that would echo throughout the ages. Such is not the case. All that is known concerning the man Methuselah through the Old Testament is that he lived and died.

Even modern-day revelation, through the writings of Moses, do him no justice. We know that he was not taken with his father Enoch, so that the Lord might fulfill His promise to Enoch, a promise that man would be saved through his loins. History reveals that Noah came through Methuselah's line, and this seems to be all we really know about him.

By contrast, even a brief life can be abundant in its quality. Quality versus quantity can be compared philosophically to knowledge and wisdom. Having an expanded intellect does not necessarily mean that wisdom also exists. This is evidenced by Paul's punctuation of man's perilous existence in these latter days, saying men would be "ever learning and never able to come to a knowledge of the truth" (2 Timothy 3:7).

Wisdom comes from knowing how to apply knowledge that one possesses, be it great or small. Likewise, a quantity of years, or possessions, does not necessarily bring quality to life. A quality life is evidenced by an ability to take what little that may be offered or available and make the most of it, whether it be time, talents, resources, knowledge, or possessions, not only for our own benefit but also for the benefit of others.

Of course, the Lord's life stands alone as the example of a quality life. Little is known of the Lord's early years, and almost nothing exists of his preparatory years leading up to his saving ministry.

We catch but a glimpse of his nature and character even as a young boy teaching the elders in the temple. Even at a tender age he knew of his divine calling, as we read his response to the concern of Joseph and Mary:

> And he said unto them, how is it that ye sought me? Wist ye not that I must be about my father's business? (Luke 2:49)

The Lord's mortal ministry spanned a short three years. These were years spent in an expression of self-mastery and the service of others, culminated by his atoning sacrifice that we might live again. Within those brief years, the Lord accomplished more than any man could have. Not even with the years of Methuselah could any man make a more significant contribution of quality to the world, and the perfect life Christ led serves as a testimony that his unrecorded years were spent in pursuit of quality. We gain further insight as to his accomplishments by John's hyperbolic statement to emphasize his glorious works:

> And there are also many other things which Jesus did, the which, if they should be written every one, I suppose that even the world itself could not contain the books that should be written. Amen. (John 21:25)

The Lord Jesus Christ stands as a standard of measure for quality. We might ask ourselves, are we striving to measure up to that standard?

Today, advances in medical technology prolong our lives, while automation allows for more free time. We must ask ourselves if our lives are dominated by the pursuit of self-indulgence, or self-mastery and self-improvement. This kind of introspection beckons a measurement of character and integrity, for a simple toss of the rare ancient coin to see which side comes up will not do. It takes a conscious, focused decision to fill our days, weeks, months, and years with the pursuit of quality through self-mastery, rather than a wish for quantity that ultimately can result in a lack of control over emotions, passions, and appetites. Isn't it interesting how a pursuit of quantity brings a sense of lacking?

Our families, careers, communities, and nations cry for us to enrich them with contributions that will endure by the virtue of the quality of our lives through self-mastery. The Lord loves to bless and prosper those who seek after self-mastery because they are seeking after Him.

Principle to Live By

If we seek for self-mastery, we will find discipline
and control to receive more and greater blessings
from God that will allow us to make contributions
in life that are fulfilling and remembered.

15

Blessing the Squirrel

Seeking God's will

Working for the Church Education System has required us to move at times to fill new assignments. One of our most cherished assignments was in Los Angeles County, where we lived in the rural setting of the Santa Clarita Valley in the hills above the San Fernando Valley. For the eight years we lived there, my wife worked as a park ranger and rehab specialist for Fish and Game. We rehabbed just about every kind of animal and bird at home you can imagine. It was a wonderful way to raise our children that instilled in them a love for nature and animals.

My wife, Tina, became very well known in the area as the "animal lady." She was in the newspaper, on the news, giving animal presentations at schools and to the public; she loved it and was good at it.

Over time, our doorbell would occasionally ring, and people would ask if she was the lady who saved animals and set them free. They all had some animal that had been injured, and they wanted to make sure it was fixed and released back into the wild. Usually, Tina would take the animal, assuring that she would do what she could to return it to nature. On some occasions, however, after assessing the animal, she would have to put the animal in our freezer, which is a very humane way of putting it out of its misery; they slowly fall asleep by freezing. Sounds cruel, but it is very humane.

For me, it was often a shock to come home and open the freezer or fridge for something to eat and see a frozen or thawing animal poised in a weird position staring back at you.

One afternoon I picked up my young daughter, Shea, from school and drove her to one of the nature centers where my wife was working that day. As we entered the nature center road, something flashed in front of the car and I swerved to miss the animal, but to my daughter it looked like I was trying to hit the creature. My daughter cried out, "What was that, Dad? Did you try to run over it?"

I stopped the car and looked in the rearview mirror to see a small animal in the road. I told my daughter to stay in front seat of the car and wait for me as I went to check on the injured animal. When I got to it, lying in the middle of the road was a large squirrel that was twitching uncontrollably. I could see the tire mark where I ran over the poor creature; I knew it was a goner. My first reaction was to pick it up by the tail and throw it in the bushes on the side of the road. As I started to reach down I looked up and saw my daughter now in the backseat with a horrified look on her face and realized I could not do that with her watching.

I stood there for a moment and thought about my options. I could pick it up, put it in the car, and take it to my wife, who could maybe help it, which might make my daughter feel better, but then I realized she would just put it in the freezer and then feed it to the fifteen-foot python named Graham. And it would be even more traumatic for my daughter to see this injured animal in our car. I stood there for a few minutes, not knowing what to do.

Finally, I started toward the car with the idea to leave it there, go drop my daughter off, and then return to toss the little guy in the bushes without her around. Suddenly, I pictured in my mind another car coming along and making a bigger mess of the situation by running over it again. I was stuck! What could I possibly do to soften the blow to my daughter and convince her that I was not a callous animal killer?

As I pondered my dilemma, unexpectedly I thought to myself, *I bear the priesthood, and knowing how the Lord loves the least of His creatures, certainly it could not be wrong for me to give this squirrel a blessing. I could possibly save a creature and redeem myself in the eyes of my tender-hearted daughter. Maybe it could be a win-win situation.*

I then did something unusual. I was alone, and it was an animal, not a person, but I said a prayer over the squirrel and then evoked priesthood power to restore it. The moment I said amen, the squirrel died. I then had to pick up the animal and carefully place it in the bushes on the side of the road, just exactly what I did not want to do with my daughter looking on.

As I got in the car, my daughter was sobbing, and I couldn't find the words to adequately console her. As I dropped her off, I drove away wondering why Heavenly Father wouldn't honor such a simple desire for what I thought was a good reason in restoring an innocent animal, and in the process comforting an innocent child. Over the next week, I wondered why my desires were not realized. But the fact was that it was an accident—couldn't I just accept the fact that sometimes sad things happen and move on? Even though I know that is a part of life, I could not get over it.

Several days later I was driving somewhere, and the question came into my mind, *Remember the squirrel?* I quickly said, "Yeah, I remember the squirrel. How come you wouldn't heal that innocent animal?" My cryptic response immediately stopped any further impressions. As I settled down and apologized to my Heavenly Father for being so prideful and sarcastic, I had a quiet and yet penetrating voice in my mind say, *It had nothing to do with your worthiness or faith—you did not ask me if it was my will.* What a simple but crushing statement. I feel that the following verse fits my situation well:

> Behold this is my will; ask and ye shall receive; but men do not always do my will. (D&C 103:31)

Knowing God's will requires seeking God in prayer, and when we don't do His will, it is because we have not asked or are just flat-out rebellious. I was praying for the wrong thing, which reminds me of another scripture that identifies a pattern we must learn to follow:

> But behold, I say unto you that ye must pray always, and not faint; that ye must not perform any thing unto the Lord save in the first place ye shall pray unto the Father in the name of Christ, that he will consecrate thy performance unto thee, that thy performance may be for the welfare of thy soul. (D&C 32:9)

Now, perhaps it was foolish for me to even think of blessing a squirrel, but that is not the point. The lesson learned was that I did not seek God's will because I did not pray to know how to perform in that moment. The pattern is clear; we need to pray before we perform. So, what does this look like? Let me walk through this idea using the logic of the scriptures. In 3 Nephi 18 we can learn something interesting about the order and the pattern of prayer. Notice what must come before faith is exercised in prayer:

> Therefore ye must always pray unto the Father in my name;
>
> And whatsoever ye shall ask the Father in my name, which is right, believing that ye shall receive, behold it shall be given unto you. (3 Nephi 18:19–20)

The nuance of knowing what is right before believing is critical. It raises another question: how do you know what is right? We find the answer in another scripture, but in this next verse notice that believing is preeminent in this specific application of prayer to determine what is right:

> Ask the Father in my name in faith, believing that you shall receive, and you shall have the Holy Ghost, which manifesteth all things which are expedient unto the children of men. (D&C 18:18)

In this instance, we pray with faith for the Holy Ghost to teach us what to pray for. The word *expedient* means important and necessary. It appears we may skip a step in the pattern of asking to know God's will. Let me share an example of this idea as found in the next chapter of the Book of Mormon. After the Savior appears to the people on the American continent and chooses His leaders, on one occasion when the twelve disciples are ministering unto the people, Christ appears and commands the people and the disciples to kneel and pray. Christ then personally prays to the Father, and when He finishes He goes to the disciples and finds them continuing in prayer. Notice how their prayers are described in the following verse:

> And it came to pass that when Jesus had thus prayed unto the Father, he came unto his disciples, and behold, they did still continue, without ceasing, to pray unto him; and they did not multiply many words, for it was given unto them what they should pray, and they were filled with desire. (3 Nephi 19:24)

Did you notice how the disciples pray without stopping, and without vain repetition of thoughts and words because the Holy Ghost is giving them the words to speak? What they are praying for is right because it is from the Spirit, even though they are doing something so unusual as praying unto Christ and not the Father (see v. 22). This is no mistake; it is a Spirit-driven experience and for whatever reason was acceptable.

When we pray with faith for the Holy Ghost to influence us, we will know what is right, and when we pray for what we desire, we can know it is God's will and we will be confident we are desiring something important and necessary for His work. And ultimately, God's work is us, so it is always important and necessary.

Strange as it may be that I desired to bless the squirrel, if I had followed the pattern and prayed first for the Spirit to tell me what to pray for, and if I felt impressed to bless that animal, I could have done so with confidence that I was doing the right thing. It matters not that it was a strange thing; if Spirit-driven, it is the right thing to do. The squirrel is not the real story here, but rather that I did not follow the prescribed pattern for seeking God's will. Pray to know what is the right thing to do before performing, and then even if it seems odd or unreasonable, you can know it is God's will.

Principle to Live By

If we learn to pray for what is right before we seek our own desires, we will know God's will in all matters and our efforts will be blessed, for us and for the benefit of others.

16

THE HUMMINGBIRD AND SHOWER OF WATER

Being immersed in the living waters of scripture

I love to work in the yard, and I love just the general feel of being outside. I especially love roses. At one time, we lived in a small custom-built home in San Diego County with a backyard that butted up to the Cleveland National Forest. The views were spectacular, and they varied at different times of the day. The previous owner had planted an English garden on the side of the house that was filled with different-colored roses. I once counted over thirty rose bushes in our yard. I watered that garden by hand, because I loved standing there, taking in the view and watching the hummingbirds that would frequent our flower garden.

One day as I was watering my roses, I noticed a specific hummingbird flying around me, and I watched it fly off and quickly return. I could tell by its color and markings it was the same little hummer. I watched a pattern develop as this hummingbird would return and each time fly closer to the water then zip away and quickly return. I thought that the hummer must be thirsty and was trying to get up the courage to take a drink, so I stood very still, not moving the water stream. Suddenly this tiny hummer landed on my thumb on the top of the nozzle. I was so shocked and excited I started to laugh nervously and shake slightly. I was so worried I would scare this little guy away, but he just sat there looking at the water and then flew away.

A few minutes later I had moved my watering position to other roses when the same hummer returned and started to circle around the shower of water and quickly dipped its beak in the outer edges of the water flow. Suddenly, this little guy dove right into the center of the shower of water and just as quickly got blasted out of the stream and flew to a branch of our small tree and sat there shaking the water off. For a few moments, it seemed that the hummer was just sitting there looking very satisfied, and then it flew away and did not return. I thought about what had just happened and I saw a correlation between us, the water, and the hummingbird.

I suppose in my experience I could represent the Lord offering His living water, and the hummer could represent us. The Lord patiently offers His living water to anyone who will come and partake of it, and it is always available. Unfortunately, some people never even notice the water. Others may come and look casually but never partake. Still others will occasionally sip of the water from its edges. And then there are those who, like this little bird, completely immerse themselves in the water and come out nourished and refreshed, perhaps even a little surprised by the result of diving in. The invitation to be immersed in the word is clearly found in the scriptures:

> Angels speak by the power of the Holy Ghost; wherefore, they speak the words of Christ. Wherefore, I said unto you, feast upon the words of Christ; for behold, the words of Christ will tell you all things what ye should do. (2 Nephi 32:3)

The word *feast* carries with it powerful imagery. Perhaps a crude analogy can be found in the difference between eating two Jack tacos for a buck and enjoying a Thanksgiving meal. Both meals can be satisfying in their own way based upon the circumstances. As a teenager, after a day at the beach, a quick pick up of the tacos was always a cheap and enjoyable end to my day in the sun and water.

By comparison, the Thanksgiving meal includes sights, sounds, smells, people, and time, and the leftovers are enjoyed for days. From this comparison we might measure our own scripture study. Do we get a buck worth out of our study, or do we get a meal out of it that lasts long after we put the scriptures down? Don't get me wrong, sometimes there is only time for the two cheap tacos, and it still can be somewhat satisfying. It should not be the norm, but if we are honest, it often is the quick fix study for many.

Having said this, perhaps what is more important than how long we study is the idea that we are feasting during the time we have. A colleague once pointed out a wonderful guiding acronym for the word FEAST: Find, Explain, Apply, Share, and Testify. If our study is to fit this acronym, we should be reading looking for doctrines and principles. When we find them, we should ponder on what they mean, find relevance considering how we can apply it, and then think of how we would share it with others. Finally, we testify of its truthfulness. Now that is feasting, and it feels like that might take time.

Considering how busy we can be in today's world, let me share a divine doctrinal truth: the Holy Ghost is faster and smarter than we are, so it matters less how long we study and more that the Spirit is involved. When He is invited into our experience, we can FEAST even in a short period of time. Remember, it did not take long for that little hummingbird to be nourished and refreshed once it dove in. Don't just sip; dive in and be immersed in the scriptures until you feel full and refreshed.

Principle to Live By

When we are determined to FEAST upon the scriptures
by immersing ourselves with the Spirit as our guide,
we will be nourished and refreshed by the Lord's
living water, and we will want to return to it again.

17

My Son's Unsafe Mission

Learning to pray differently

When my son Dane was called on a mission to Monterrey, Mexico, we thought how it sounded like such a beautiful, exotic place. It was even immortalized in a song by Frank Sinatra. We were so excited for him, but as we talked about his mission with family, we discovered that the mission took in all the border towns across from Texas where the drug cartels, military, and competition were killing one another and innocent people over control of the drug trade into the United States. Some of these towns were in fact very violent and dangerous. Some of our family felt a real and understandable concern that we would send our son into such a dangerous situation for two years. One of our family members worked in law enforcement as a career and had friends and contacts with the DEA and Homeland Security as well as other entities.

As Dane got in the mission field and we started to hear about some of the struggles that he had, we became more concerned. There was some banter back and forth between us and one of our in-the-know loved ones about how if things got too dangerous he would have friends pull Dane out of the mission field to safety. We felt it was serious enough that we told him, "If you take Dane out, you must take his companion with him as well—it is a mission rule that they can't be left alone!" This was said in humor, I'm sure, but with undertones of seriousness. I had visions of black ops flying in with a helicopter, whisking Dane away to safety on a hanging rope ladder from the whirlybird while his companion looked up in horror.

As Dane's mission progressed, we learned that he and his companion were caught in the middle of a shoot-out between the cartel and some local enemies, and he and his companion had to crawl to the safety of a member's home. On another occasion, they were moved late one night on the spur of the moment because they had been threatened by the Mexican mafia. There were several other instances where their safety was in question, but suffice it to say, we as a family were very concerned, although Dane said he always felt safe. Our anxiety increased as emails got shorter and several times never came on the scheduled day.

Anyway, a kind of anxiousness just always hung around, and even though we prayed for his safety and I believed the Lord would protect my son, I never found the peace that I desired and needed as a parent who felt helpless as my son was so far away.

About six months into my son's mission, I still was not finding peace, so I started to ask in prayer what I needed to do to find the peaceful feelings I so yearned for. At this point my prayers were always a plea that Heavenly Father and the Lord would protect Elder Raleigh, not uncommon to what every good parent or family member would do for their missionary child—or for that matter, any child who was away from home. Over time, I started to receive impressions that I should pray differently. I did not know what that meant or how to do it, so I eventually was reminded of a previous principle I taught about praying first for the Spirit to teach me what to pray for. Remember these verses used earlier:

> Ask the Father in my name in faith, believing that you shall receive, and you shall have the Holy Ghost, which manifesteth all things which are expedient unto the children of men. (D&C 18:18)

> And it came to pass that when Jesus had thus prayed unto the Father, he came unto his disciples, and behold, they did still

> continue, without ceasing, to pray unto him; and they did not multiply many words, for it was given unto them what they should pray, and they were filled with desire. (3 Nephi 19:24)

What I love about 3 Nephi 19:24 is the phrase "they were filled with desire." That is what I wanted for me and my wife, to pray with the Spirit with approved desire that would bring peace to my soul. As I continued to pray for my son's safety, I also prayed to be inspired on how to pray differently. Eventually, I came to understand that I needed to pray in language of gratitude. What this meant for me was discovered one night as I prayed under the influence of the Spirit and was filled with a great unspoken desire, and I was surprised with what I said. Compare the following language of my prayers:

> "Heavenly Father, please protect my son today."

Compared to:

> "Heavenly Father, I thank thee for protecting my son today as thou hast every day while he has been serving the Lord in the mission field. I am grateful unto thee for this blessing and for the peace it brings to me and my family."

It was just a simple adjustment; rather than asking, I was thanking my Heavenly Father for the very things I desired. As I thought about what happened in my prayer, I realized I was still in a sense asking and relying upon divine protection for my son, but the shift in language now also blessed me with the peace that my son would be safe no matter what was happening. My son's safety was not based solely on my asking daily for his protection; certainly the Lord desired to protect His young servant who had sacrificed so much, and willingly, to go to a place that was not comfortable, convenient, or peaceful. What the Lord desired was beyond my own desires, and He also wanted my wife and me, as well as our loved ones, to find peace in the service that he was rendering, and not just to have a hope that he would be protected from danger.

I am in awe of the Lord's goodness, power, and mercy in my life and the lives of those I love. He is so kind and patient as I stumble along in life until I learn further soul-expanding principles that bless my life and the lives of so many others. I love the idea that I was in my fifties before I learned that I could still improve my prayers, and I am anxious to continue to be perfected in the basic principles of the Lord's gospel. Couching our prayers in language of gratitude can make all the difference.

Principle to Live By

If we learn to pray with language of gratitude,
we will find peace along with the blessings we so
desperately desire for ourselves and others.

18

Going Out for Dessert in Embarrassing Clothes

Always be prepared

Emergency preparedness and provident living are things Latter-day Saints, along with so many other good people, believe are important principles in today's world. When it was just me and my wife, we didn't feel the anxiousness or motivation to store food, water, money, clothes, supplies, etc. It wasn't until several years after Dane was born that we felt a need to do something.

When my son was about three or four years old, Tina had us collect a change of clothes, some canned goods, water, matches, candles, flashlights, blankets, and other sundry items to put in a big trunk that we would store in the garage for emergencies that we honestly felt probably would never come.

The years flew by, we now had a sweet daughter, and life seemed great. I never thought of the trunk except when we had to move into a new home. That trunk was a beast to pick up and move around, so we would find a good place in the garage and use it to stack other things on, never really giving it much thought otherwise.

One Monday night for family home evening, my wife had a brilliant idea. As we all gathered together, she announced that we just had an emergency earthquake and we needed to go get our supplies and head out. We went to the garage to find that old rusty trunk full of our survival supplies. The kids were excited, and I was thinking this is a clever way to teach our children about preparedness. A phrase from a scripture popped into my mind:

> But if ye are prepared ye shall not fear. (D&C 38:30)

I felt good about us as a family; I felt we were prepared. We located the trunk and removed all the junk on top of it. It was so filthy with dirt, grime, and rust from years of garage life. I am not sure what was in some of those boxes stacked on top of it, but man, it was sticky and gooey with gunk on top of it—I did not want to touch it!

When we finally got it open and started to remove the canned food, we discovered some of the cans had swollen and were leaking; there was no way anyone was going to be eating that can of stew. What a waste! I even had a set of scriptures in there that looked like they shrunk and were warped with pages stuck together. So far, no food and no spiritual nourishment. This was not good.

As we continued to dig through the stuff and be grossed out, we found the ultimate insult, our reserved set of clothes. Tina had us put on our emergency clothes in the garage. It was hilarious! First of all, Shea wasn't even born when we made up the trunk, so there were no clothes for her. And then Dane put on an outfit that consisted of a bright pink pair of funky sweatpants that barely made it to his waist with the bottoms hitting him mid-calf. Then he put on a yellow Ninja-Turtle T-shirt that didn't even cover his midsection. Shrunken pink pants and yellow super-hero T-shirt—YIKES! I even felt embarrassed for him.

I turned to look at Tina's outfit, and although it was out of style, it fit her perfectly and she looked okay. Now it was my turn. I pulled on a pair of brown corduroy pants that were so tight, and as I shimmied them up I couldn't button them and was only able to zip them about three-quarters of the way up. It was so uncomfortable, not just the pants but especially my ego. I then pulled out the shirt.

I loved that shirt, and I still have it in my personal history bin today, but for the life of me I can't understand why in the world I would choose that heavy, unusual-looking shirt as my go-to wardrobe if bad things broke loose.

As we stood there looking at each other, we started laughing at one another, and then we realized how actually unprepared we really were. Tina then gave a simple lesson to our children of how being prepared can make us happy. We were laughing at each other but were not happy about how we felt.

Good one, Tina—lesson learned! Then Tina said, "Okay let's get in the car and go get a treat." I thought she was kidding, but she wasn't. I told her there was no way we were going out in public looking like that. We finally agreed to go to a drive-thru, but we were still embarrassed as the food was passed through the window to a family that was dressed in outdated, obnoxiously colored, and poorly fitting clothes. It was one of the best family home evenings we ever had, and we laugh about that experience still today.

What a great lesson for us to learn. We often think we are prepared for the unexpected, and we may even trust others to make sure we are prepared, when in fact family preparation begins with individual preparation. The scriptures teach this principle clearly in the Doctrine and Covenants as the Lord makes this point using a parable of a nobleman who commands his servants to plant olive trees and then build a tower to watch over it so the fruit of his vineyard is not spoiled:

> Now, the servants of the nobleman went and did as their lord commanded them, and planted the olive trees, and built a hedge round about, and set watchmen, and began to build a tower.
>
> And while they were yet laying the foundation thereof, they began to say among themselves: And what need hath my lord of this tower?
>
> And consulted for a long time, saying among themselves: What need hath my lord of this tower, seeing this is a time of peace?

> Might not this money be given to the exchangers? For there is no need of these things.
>
> And while they were at variance one with another they became very slothful, and they hearkened not unto the commandments of their lord.
>
> And the enemy came by night, and broke down the hedge; and the servants of the nobleman arose and were affrighted, and fled; and the enemy destroyed their works, and broke down the olive trees.
>
> Now, behold, the nobleman, the lord of the vineyard, called upon his servants, and said unto them, Why! what is the cause of this great evil?
>
> Ought ye not to have done even as I commanded you, and—after ye had planted the vineyard, and built the hedge round about, and set watchmen upon the walls thereof—built the tower also, and set a watchman upon the tower, and watched for my vineyard, and not have fallen asleep, lest the enemy should come upon you?
>
> And behold, the watchman upon the tower would have seen the enemy while he was yet afar off; and then ye could have made ready and kept the enemy from breaking down the hedge thereof, and saved my vineyard from the hands of the destroyer. (D&C 101:44–54)

At times, we may not see a reason or even understand why we are asked to prepare for things that present no real need now, or even in the perceived near future. Like in the parable, we can become slothful in our preparations by either doing nothing, not finishing it, or not updating it. Real preparation requires continual effort and watching. Simply packing and waiting won't do. Understanding why we need to be prepared helps us count the cost of our efforts now and for the future. This idea is accentuated in the New Testament:

> For which of you, intending to build a tower, sitteth not down first, and counteth the cost, whether he have sufficient to finish it? (Luke 14:28)

Counting the cost and finishing requires anticipation and a willingness to be perpetually and adequately prepared for anything that may come. As we all know, challenges and emergencies aren't calendared; they just happen. We also need to make sure the preparations actually "fit" the potential unplanned problems that can arise quickly and unexpectedly.

As important as preparation is for unwelcome events, it is also critical for those most important and anticipated experiences we yearn for. This kind of preparation is best described in the parable of the Ten Virgins. Notice what constitutes real preparation in this parable:

> Then shall the kingdom of heaven be likened unto ten virgins, which took their lamps, and went forth to meet the bridegroom.
>
> And five of them were wise, and five were foolish.
>
> They that were foolish took their lamps, and took no oil with them:
>
> But the wise took oil in their vessels with their lamps.
>
> While the bridegroom tarried, they all slumbered and slept.
>
> And at midnight there was a cry made, Behold, the bridegroom cometh; go ye out to meet him.
>
> Then all those virgins arose, and trimmed their lamps.
>
> And the foolish said unto the wise, Give us of your oil; for our lamps are gone out.
>
> But the wise answered, saying, Not so; lest there be not enough for us and you: but go ye rather to them that sell, and buy for yourselves.
>
> And while they went to buy, the bridegroom came; and they that were ready went in with him to the marriage: and the door was shut.
>
> Afterward came also the other virgins, saying, Lord, Lord, open to us.
>
> But he answered and said, Verily I say unto you, I know you not.
>
> Watch therefore, for ye know neither the day nor the hour wherein the Son of man cometh. (Matt. 25:1–13)

Appropriate preparation is a perpetual state of watching, which implies that we are doing things and adjusting those things in our lives that allow us to be prepared for an unexpected or anticipated moment. The oil represents the Holy Ghost, which comes and dwells in our lives as we do those "drop by drop" things that help us not "slumber and sleep" through the most critical moments of our lives. When the call comes, we are prepared to respond, and while we wait for the call, we are not afraid.

It is an interesting thing to me that most of our fears in life are about things that haven't even happened yet. Real preparation, physical and spiritual, brings a sense of peace and happiness that carries over into those moments of trial. We can find happiness in the idea that we are prepared for those intrusions into our lives that are uninvited and unwelcome and still find joy for being prepared for those times, as well as for those things we look forward to. Live by the principle of anticipation rather than desperation.

Principle to Live By

Learn to count the cost, and then do the things that will prepare us for the future and find happiness and peace in our preparedness.

19

The Gift of Tongues

Be careful of private interpretation

When our children were young, I had a time-consuming calling along with a busy career and all the responsibilities that come from being a husband and a father. One day, while focused on my busy life, I had the impression to seek after the gift of tongues. This was shocking to me because foreign languages and I don't get along.

Prior to going on my mission, back in the day, they would give you a language aptitude test, and I failed miserably. I was fortunate enough to still serve in a foreign land and speak English; I went to England, and Cockney was as foreign to me as any other language. The only real time in my life I had even studied a language was in high school when I took French because there was a cute girl in that class that I wanted to get to know.

Thinking back, I did take Spanish for a year in preparation to go to Honduras with a service organization when I was sixteen, but I found it was useless when I got down there and found they spoke a variation of Spanish slang. The fact that I grew up in San Diego and did not master the Spanish language tells you something about me. Anyway, I can't learn or speak other languages; let's leave it at that.

The fact that I hadn't shown a capacity to learn another language made some sense in a weird way for me to seek for the gift of tongues, because I would need divine help in doing so. But I did not know why, and that caused me more anxiety than having to learn a language. I started to speculate that maybe Tina and I would be called to serve a mission, and so I lumped Tina in with me on the idea that "we" needed to start learning a language—but what language?

I spent months trying to figure out what language we should study; I even made it a matter of fasting and prayer but never got an answer, not even a hint. I would go to bookstores and stand at the foreign language section trying to get some inclination of a language that would make an impression upon me, but still nothing came.

This in no way deterred me from my divinely mandated mission to seek after the gift of tongues so we could be prepared when that anticipated call would come to serve a mission for the Church. However, my excitement was muted by the frustration I felt after months of searching, and I still had no idea of the direction we should go.

One day, while expressing my frustration with trying to figure out what language we should learn, something unexpected happened that was not only offensive but profound. Tina looked at me and said, "Honey, do you know what the gift of tongues is for you?"

The way she spoke in the form of a question got my attention, but the tone was interesting, so I responded slowly and sheepishly, "What?" She responded quickly and pointedly, "You need to learn to teach your children in family home evening so they can understand you," and then she turned and walked away. Was my wife telling me I was a poor teacher, or that I did not use the English language well in my teaching? I wasn't sure, but I was offended! Then the Spirit washed over me, and I knew she was right.

Wow, I was way off in my thinking. I wondered why the Lord didn't just give me that insight many months before so I didn't waste my time trying to figure out what that impression meant. He could have spared me the embarrassment of finding out I was a horrible teacher to my children, although, deep inside, I already knew that I was. But that is a hard thing for an institute director and religious educator to admit. I was good at teaching everyone else's kids but not my own. What a blow to my ego.

If I am honest, our family home evenings were a nightmare, not because of my children but because of my unrealistic expectations. I expected my children to act and respond as my institute students did, and so I was always so impatient and frustrated. My wife, however, was so good at teaching our children. Thank goodness for good women in our lives who teach our children well.

I learned a great lesson from that experience. On occasion, in our lives we may receive impressions that we can easily misinterpret if we are not careful. When we receive what we think and feel are spiritually driven impressions, we would be wise to go to our Heavenly Father in prayer to verify if they are indeed from Him. Once verified, we can pursue clarification as to their intended meaning and its application in our lives. When we have an incorrect understanding, we are apt to put a value or interpretation on its meaning that may be way out in left field. I have learned that the Lord will test us in this way with a well-timed revelation to see what value or meaning we will attach to our experience. Let me share the context of an example from 1 Kings in the Old Testament to make my point.

The Lord sends a prophet from Judah to the northern kingdom to call Jeroboam to repentance for idolatry. In the exchange between the two men, Jeroboam is upset with the prophet, and as he reaches out in anger, his hand is withered. He petitions the prophet to ask the Lord to heal him, and in mercy the Lord does restore his hand. Out of gratitude, Jeroboam invites the prophet to come home with him to be refreshed, but he refuses because of the commandment he received from the Lord. Notice what happens to the prophet of Judah when another prophet invites him to come home with him, and consider how what happens to him teaches the lesson we are considering:

> And went after the man of God, and found him sitting under an oak: and he said unto him, Art thou the man of God that camest from Judah? And he said, I am.
>
> Then he said unto him, Come home with me, and eat bread.
>
> And he said, I may not return with thee, nor go in with thee: neither will I eat bread nor drink water with thee in this place:
>
> For it was said to me by the word of the Lord, Thou shalt eat no bread nor drink water there, nor turn again to go by the way that thou camest.
>
> He said unto him, I am a prophet also as thou art; and an angel spake unto me by the word of the Lord, saying, Bring him back with thee into thine house, that he may eat bread and drink water. But he lied unto him. (See Joseph Smith Translation footnote).
>
> So he went back with him, and did eat bread in his house, and drank water.
>
> And it came to pass, as they sat at the table, that the word of the Lord came unto the prophet that brought him back:
>
> And he cried unto the man of God that came from Judah, saying, Thus saith the Lord, Forasmuch as thou hast disobeyed the mouth of the Lord, and hast not kept the commandment which the Lord thy God commanded thee,
>
> But camest back, and hast eaten bread and drunk water in the place, of the which the Lord did say to thee, Eat no bread, and drink no water; thy carcase shall not come unto the sepulchre of thy fathers.
>
> And it came to pass, after he had eaten bread, and after he had drunk, that he saddled for him the ass, to wit, for the prophet whom he had brought back.
>
> And when he was gone, a lion met him by the way, and slew him: and his carcase was cast in the way, and the ass stood by it, the lion also stood by the carcase. (1 Kings 13:8–30)

This may seem a harsh punishment from the Lord upon this prophet from Judah, but it teaches a great lesson about the importance of verifying with the Lord before we move forward with the wrong interpretation. Learning to value the Lord's commandments according to His will is critical to our salvation. We see such contradictions in the world today between man's interpretation of God's will and what He really desires of us in the form of His salvation. I don't believe that prophet lost his exaltation, but he did suffer a harsh consequence in mortality and lost further opportunities here.

From a modern-day, Western Hemisphere perspective this does not sound fair, but from an ancient-world and eternal perspective it is effective in teaching us the importance of seeking God's will in all things. It is important to point out that the Joseph Smith Translation of 1 Kings 13:18 restores lost truth to the verse. It should read:

> . . . drink water, that I may prove him; and he lied not unto him.

The phrases "that I may prove him" and "he lied not" are critical to understanding the moral of this story. Although this feels like such a contradiction to the command the prophet of Judah received from the Lord not to stop in that land but return home without haste, when we understand that the Lord proves His people, and at times in unusual circumstances, then there is no contradiction here. Simply stated, if the prophet from Judah had verified the new command with the Lord, whatever the Lord told him would be the right thing to do, even if it countermanded what he was previously told to do.

So how is this relevant to our day? Let me use myself as an example of what many of you may have already experienced. There have been several instances where a bishopric or stake presidency was changed and out of the blue I received impressions that I would be called to be a bishop or to serve in a stake presidency. After the initial shock wore off, I would start to think about who I would call to serve with me or what our focus for the ward or stake would be. These are normal things to consider if indeed that were true.

However, when I was not called, I started to question my ability to receive inspiration and beat myself up for aspiring to a calling, as well as wondering how susceptible I was to the adversary's influence. Again, I was putting the wrong interpretation and value upon what didn't happen.

I eventually learned that the Lord never said I would be the *next* bishop or serve in the *next* stake presidency. I made that assumption. The Lord just happened to use that moment to throw out an impression to see what I would do with it. Unfortunately, I failed, but I learned from those experiences so I might not make the same mistake again. Like the prophet from Judah, I never went to the Lord for verification, and as a result, I was open to all kinds of interesting thoughts that caused wonderment and frustration.

Years later, I had some things clarified when my brother was called as a bishop, and the stake president, after announcing the new bishopric, taught the congregation that there were multiple men in that audience who had received impressions that they would be called as the bishop, and now they were struggling with the fact that they were not called. He explained that the Lord wanted them to know they were worthy, and the day would come when they would be called, just not then. What an interesting way to send a message. I also believe the timing of the impression was to teach a further lesson on how to receive revelation from the Lord. Notice the doctrinal teaching in the following verses:

> Knowing this first, that no prophecy of the scripture is of any private interpretation.
>
> For the prophecy came not in old time by the will of man: but holy men of God spake as they were moved by the Holy Ghost. (2 Peter 1:20–21)

Like scripture, revelation that flows from God cannot be opened to our own private interpretation. If it comes through the Spirit, it requires that we verify it by the Spirit. We must remember it is a multifaceted process of verifying, then clarifying. This is the Lord's way, and we need to follow the process no matter how long that may take. Learn to receive, verify, and then clarify.

Principle to Live By

Learn to verify impressions from the Lord and to seek further insights rather than putting our own interpretation and value on its meaning. Then continue to ask if there is more to understand.

20

Peas Don't Flush Easily

Honesty is best

I don't like peas, lima beans, or any other food that is green with a pasty feel to it. In fact, I did not purposely chew a pea until I was twenty-three and on my mission, and even then it just verified my distaste for peas.

My distaste started when I was about eight. My mother remarried, and it pains me to say this, but for a time I did not like my stepfather for a couple of reasons. One, he was a dentist—what kid likes dentists? And two, he made us eat weird food.

My dentist dad was a health nut in terms of food and exercise. Not only did we not have candy around the house, we also had to eat tons of veggies and at times weird, disgusting stuff for a kid.

Unfortunately, my stepfather was a man I did not learn to appreciate fully until he was gone. He passed away when I was eighteen or nineteen from cancer. But while he was with us, he was strict on what we ate. Every meal was accompanied with multiple vegetables that were always the things I disliked most, and peas always seemed to be a staple with our meals. To make it worse, there was no dessert until I ate all the food on my plate. What a dilemma. How do I get around the bad food, so I can get the good food—dessert?

For a time, I tried drinking water with each mouthful to wash it down without chewing. By the time I finished drinking my peas down, I just felt sick and could not eat anything else. However, if

I tried eating my meal first and then finished it off with the water-logged peas sliding into my belly, I felt like throwing up. Either way I was guaranteed a miserable meal experience.

In desperation, I came up with an idea. I would take a mouthful of peas and slide them with my tongue to the side of my mouth and pretend to chew my food. Then at an unsuspecting moment I would take my napkin and pretend to wipe my mouth while spitting the peas into it. Once one napkin was full, I would tuck it into the waistband of my pants for disposal later. Because of this technique, I started wearing loose-fitting pants to accomplish my well-thought-out plan because I needed room for multiple napkins filled with those green demons.

I had to be very careful. After doing this for a time I started to feel uneasy and knew that odds were at some point I was going to get nailed by my parents or my siblings, who would use this against me at some future day when I ticked them off—it would become their leverage against me.

As I thought about what I could do to change up the discarding of the peas, I thought I would try flushing them down the toilet. Brilliant! No witnesses and no evidence. By the way, at this point I was really good at getting the peas into my napkins undetected. However, my first attempt with this new technique was a disaster. I got the peas into the napkins with no problem and got them into the bathroom, which was located just off the kitchen. I thought things were going to be so easy, but there was an unanticipated problem.

I emptied the peas into the toilet and then flushed. The whirlpool got those peas moving in a circular motion and they went down with the water. As I started to close the lid thinking I was home free, I looked down and something shocking happened: the peas came back up with the refill. I thought maybe I did not hold down the handle long enough to make sure it picked up more pressure to take the peas seaward. I waited for the tank to refill so I could try holding the handle down longer until it completely emptied the reserve tank of water. The whirlpool looked like it had greater power this time, and I was sure it would take the peas away forever. Then, as the water pushed itself upward, there were about half the peas still floating on top of the water. I was dumbfounded.

Each flush did take a few more away, but it was taking longer and longer between flushes and I was flushing like crazy. By this time, my mother, who was in the kitchen, heard my multiple flushes and thought something was wrong. Her motherly inclinations sensed a child was having intestinal problems and came to knock on the door and ask if I was okay. I responded that I was fine as I flushed again. By now my mom knew something fishy was going on and demanded I open the door. I just had a few more peas to dispose of and stopped responding to her while I frantically was flushing without waiting.

Suddenly I heard my stepdad demand I open the door, and I knew a severe punishment was eminent if I didn't, so I unlocked the door, closed the lid on the toilet, and sat down.

My parents came in and demanded I tell them what was going on. I tried to hide my actions with a stupid lame lie that I found someone had dumped their peas in the toilet, and I was trying to flush them, so they didn't get in trouble. Now I was blaming one of my siblings and trying to make myself look good in some way. They saw right through me, and I knew they would think of some "distasteful" punishment, like making me eat a double portion of peas right there. However, my punishment did not have anything to do with food. What made it worse was that my parents told me if I was just honest with them they wouldn't be mad with me and I would have avoided a severe punishment.

My parents had moved from the corporal punishment of spanking to the lengthy experience of writing a designated phrase anywhere from one hundred to one thousand times, depending on how bad the act was. The phrase went something like this: "I will not throw away my food and lie about it."

So, was flushing the peas that big of a deal? After all, what kid at some time in their life has not tried to throw away something they disliked? Yes, it was wasteful, but more importantly I was dishonest about it, and when I was ultimately caught, I continued to try and hide my dishonesty by involving someone else in the mix, in this case blaming an innocent someone else.

What I learned from the pea-flushing experience is that if I had just been just upfront and honest with my parents, they would have been far more merciful and patient with my indiscretions. The ultimate solution, of course, was simple: just eat the darn peas. However, being deceitful in my attempt to discard the evidence followed up with a dishonest effort to hide the wrongdoing just magnified my youthful stupidity and the punishment.

I remember even on my mission, when it came to peas and brussels sprouts, which were so common in England, I went as far as to say that I was allergic to them but that my companion loved them. That was not true on both counts. Bad habits die slowly. Don't get me wrong, I still will not consciously chew a pea. I won't drink them down or discard them in a wasteful way. Now I just refuse to eat them under all circumstances, and I don't feel bad about it.

In how many ways do we find ourselves being untruthful with actions or excuses if we don't want to do something? It does not have to be distasteful to us; it can just be inconvenient, uncomfortable, or not appealing to us at that moment. And the worst part is that we don't feel it is being dishonest. Sometimes we may even recruit others to help us sell our excuses as to why we can't participate. If I am honest, I can still find times in my life when I return to my pea-flushing experience, and somehow feel like I am not being dishonest, but rather just trying not to offend someone with my refusal. The Lord said it simply:

> And let every man deal honestly, and be alike among this people, and receive alike, that ye may be one, even as I have commanded you. (D&C 51:9)

I know honestly is the best policy, because eventually we will get caught. The question is *What do we do then?* Remember, untruths and half-truths, like peas, don't flush easily, and we compound the problem by trying to excuse our lies with further dishonesty. Be honest in all things, so we can be one with God and our fellow men.

Principle to Live By

When we learn to be honest, even in the little things, we become one with the Lord, our loved ones, and our fellow men.

21

Riding Bikes with Friends

Not leaving others behind

As a young boy, my younger brother Mike was my best friend. We did everything together, and living in the rural part of the county was a great place for young adventurous boys to live. We played all over the vacant fields and open areas, staying close enough to hear our mom call us home.

Because I am two years older than my brother, I learned to do things several years before him. This was not a problem until one day when some of the neighborhood boys asked me if I wanted to go exploring on our bikes. I was so excited because I had never been exploring on my bike before, and I was never invited to hang out with this group of older boys, who seemed so cool.

I immediately said yes and went to get permission and my adventuring stuff. I grabbed something to eat for the trip and headed out the front door, jumping over my brother, who was sitting on the front porch, to get my bike out of the garage. I was ready to go.

As I walked my bike out of the garage, I realized something that cooled my excitement. My brother could not ride a bike, and he wasn't invited. Mike sat there looking at me with the saddest look on his little face. What a dilemma for an older brother: *Do I go do something that sounds so exciting, and almost a rite of passage for a young boy to hang out with the older guys, or do I stay with my buddy?* I felt that brotherly tug in my gut until the other boys went flying by my house on their bikes, yelling for me to get going. The adventure began, and I would have to move quickly to catch up and keep up.

With no time to think, I just reacted, jumping on my bike, and off I went. I turned back for just a moment to see my brother crying with his chin cupped in his little hands. As I pedaled frantically, standing up with my body swaying back and forth to get more power out of my legs, I suddenly did something even surprising to me. I stopped pedaling, sat down on my seat, and slowed down as I saw my brother in my mind's eye sitting there alone and sad. Then a thought came to me so subtly that I didn't recognize it as a spiritual prompting; it was just a quiet thought that there would be other days to ride with the older boys, but today my brother was alone and I needed to be with him. I just yelled to the other boys "Gotta go!" and turned my bike around.

Riding slowly back home, I felt calm, and as I got to the corner of our street and our house came into view, I could see Mike sitting there with his head down, crying, and then I had the most brilliant idea. He was so preoccupied with his sadness that he did not see me pass by our street and head for the unfenced backyard of our neighbor that allowed me to enter our backyard unseen. I would surprise my brother by coming in the back of the house and then blast out of the front door. I was able to make my way into the house undetected and prepare to astound my brother with my surprise. I quickly opened the front door and said, "Hey buddy, what are you doing?" He turned around and his face lit up with the biggest smile, and he asked me how I did that. He was so happy to see me, and it felt so good to make him smile again. I don't remember what we did that day. I just remember how good it felt to be with my brother, and I know we had a blast doing whatever it was we did.

Mike and I over the years have referred to that experience whenever we get nostalgic. Mike always reflects on how much it meant to him that his older brother would do that, and I describe how good it felt to find a way to surprise my best little buddy.

Over the years, I have pondered about things I learned from that experience. There are designated times in our lives when it is necessary to literally leave loved ones behind for work and callings and other activities. However, in those necessary moments of separation, we can take them with us mentally, emotionally, and spiritually.

As I got older, I certainly did choose my friends more often over my brother, but because of that experience, we knew how important we were to each other and we could have those separating moments, knowing it would not affect our brotherly relationship but rather enhance the fewer times we did have together. This is analogous to our experience in mortality.

Opportunities that draw our attention and excite us can become a distraction from something more important. If we are not careful in following impressions to forgo personal choices for better things, we can become desensitized until it is easy to always choose the immediately appealing opportunity.

Another lesson I learned was that at times we may feel alone or left behind like my brother, but that is just not true. Mike was in my heart, and more importantly, Mike was in the Lord's heart so much so that He prompted an older brother to return and comfort a younger brother in his time of need. Everyone's experiences will not be the same in appearance, but the truth remains constant—we are never alone; we are always in someone's heart and mind, and we are always under the Lord's gaze. He will send tender mercies to each one of us on special occasions when we need them most.

In this exciting time of change and adjustment in the Lord's work, a time when the Lord is inviting us to minister to others with love fueled by inspiration, we need to develop the ability to receive and respond to personal revelation on how we can more carefully minister the way the Lord would.

Ministering to people is so much more important than participating in activities that may be satisfying in and of themselves. However, we also can become neglectful if we always choose people over other needs. Let me share an example of how we can do both in a sense.

Going to the temple is an important and necessary thing to do, even though it does separate us physically from those we love who at times may wonder why we don't stay with them. However, we can still be connected mentally, emotionally, and spiritually with them as we go to the temple. Here is how this can be accomplished.

At a time in the life of my beautiful teenage daughter, Shea, when she experienced vulnerability and harshness from the youthful cruelty of others, I felt impressed to take her with me in my heart to the temple every time I served weekly as an ordinance worker. There were times after she had a bad day I just wanted to stay home and talk to her or just do something fun with her to make her feel better. But I knew I could not do that, so I would take Shea with me in my heart and mind to the temple. I would picture her in every room and in every ordinance performed there. In my prayers I would picture her in my mind's eye as I expressed my personal desires for her. I acted as if she were really with me there, in the temple, at that moment. It was amazing the connection I felt to her even though we were apart.

Don't get me wrong—there were times, like with my brother, I chose my children or family over the temple, or a meeting, or even a service project if I felt impressed to do so. The key to that exception comes from the Spirit. I learned many years ago to always read or listen for application and never for preference or exception. But when the Spirit offered the exception, I have tried to follow that impression, and I have found it has always been in favor of the need of an individual. In those more frequent times when the activity does take precedence over loved ones, I have tried to take them with me in a very personal and internal way. I love the Lord's example in

3 Nephi that models both sides of the issue and the importance of following spiritual impressions:

> Behold, now it came to pass that when Jesus had spoken these words he looked round about again on the multitude, and he said unto them: Behold, my time is at hand.
>
> I perceive that ye are weak, that ye cannot understand all my words which I am commanded of the Father to speak unto you at this time.
>
> Therefore, go ye unto your homes, and ponder upon the things which I have said, and ask of the Father, in my name, that ye may understand, and prepare your minds for the morrow, and I come unto you again.
>
> But now I go unto the Father, and also to show myself unto the lost tribes of Israel, for they are not lost unto the Father, for he knoweth whither he hath taken them.
>
> And it came to pass that when Jesus had thus spoken, he cast his eyes round about again on the multitude, and beheld they were in tears, and did look steadfastly upon him as if they would ask him to tarry a little longer with them.
>
> And he said unto them: Behold, my bowels are filled with compassion towards you.
>
> Have ye any that are sick among you? Bring them hither. Have ye any that are lame, or blind, or halt, or maimed, or leprous, or that are withered, or that are deaf, or that are afflicted in any manner? Bring them hither and I will heal them, for I have compassion upon you; my bowels are filled with mercy.
>
> For I perceive that ye desire that I should show unto you what I have done unto your brethren at Jerusalem, for I see that your faith is sufficient that I should heal you. (3 Nephi 17:1–8)

I find it enlightening that the Lord thought it more important in that instance to choose to stay with the people over going to His Father and fulfilling His commandment to visit the lost tribes of Israel. The Lord followed the impression to stay with the people and bless them in miraculous ways. That is what they needed at that moment and not a promised blessing tomorrow. Further in that chapter, Jesus shows that even though far away from those in

Jerusalem, who treated Him cruelly, they were still in His heart and mind, as we read:

> And it came to pass that when they had all been brought, and Jesus stood in the midst, he commanded the multitude that they should kneel down upon the ground.
>
> And it came to pass that when they had knelt upon the ground, Jesus groaned within himself, and said: Father, I am troubled because of the wickedness of the people of the house of Israel. (3 Nephi 17:13–14)

Certainly, Heavenly Father had to be pleased with His Son, who was mindful of those He was with, those He had left behind, and those He still needed to visit. His choice to minister to the immediate needs of the people was appropriate, and the Father knew His Son would ultimately be obedient to the other needful things later. The truth is that we are always in the forefront of Christ's mind.

Sometimes assignments, meetings, and reports can wait when compared to the ministering needs of others, and yet when we do need to go, we can always take loved ones, friends, and fellow saints with us in our hearts and minds.

Principle to Live By

Look for ways to minister to others, and when choices present themselves, follow the impressions that may come. When we cannot always be with them, take them with us in our minds and hearts, so no one gets left behind.

22

Rolling the Family Car into a Ravine

Learning to act and live with power

Our home had a driveway that was a long, curved road slightly slanted toward the inside bank, away from a ravine along the outside edge. The driveway rose somewhat steeply until it reached the top of the hill. At the top of the driveway and to the left was a ravine with maybe a ten- to fifteen-foot drop. It didn't look like much until you were at the bottom trying to climb back up.

As the driveway flattened out in front of the garage, it made a nice place to shoot baskets. Attached to the garage was a homemade basketball rim nailed into a piece of plywood for a backboard.

Because the basketball hoop was somewhat close to the bank, you had to develop an additional skill of being quick enough to catch up to an errant pass or a missed shot to keep the ball from rolling down the hill. After a few experiences of not being quick enough, we would just stand there on the edge and watch it roll all the way down to the canyon and then start ripping on the person who caused it. Eventually we made a rule that whoever took the errant shot or made a bad pass was responsible to go get it. Now to the story.

One Saturday afternoon, my brother and his friend wanted to shoot baskets with me. I only had on basketball shorts and tennis shoes because it was so hot. The problem was that my parents' brand-new car was parked outside of the garage in front of the basket. To this day, I honestly don't know why we did not just go ask my parents to move the car. By the way, the car had power steering and power brakes, which only worked when the car was on. And the steering wheel would lock in place when you turned it to a certain angle.

So rather than bother my parents, I just told my brother and his friend to push the car and I would steer as we backed the car out of the way to shoot baskets. I hopped in the car, put it into reverse, and told the guys to push slowly as I had my foot on the brake. At first everything was fine as the car moved slowly on the flat part of the driveway. However, as the incline of the drive increased behind me, the car picked up momentum. I pushed on the brake, and nothing happened, so I stomped again, but I wasn't strong enough to make it work. I started yelling at my brother while he was yelling back at me that my joke wasn't funny. I found out later that power brakes barely worked when the car is off. That information would have been useful before I got into the car!

As the car picked up momentum and pulled away from my brother, he mistook the panicked look on my face as a brotherly fake out. Again, he just looked at me and yelled to knock it off because it wasn't funny. Now I could see in the rearview mirror I am heading for the ravine directly behind me, and so I tried to turn the steering wheel to the right to keep from backing straight into the ravine. At that moment, it seemed like the only thing to do. Looking back, it just redirected me down the driveway.

Now I was moving in a direction that was going to take me partially downhill and into the ravine, so I yanked on the wheel and it locked in position. Again, that information could have been useful earlier. I was screaming, sweating, and shaking when I looked up and saw my brother laughing nervously at me. I was heading toward the ravine and downhill at the same time but at an angle that eventually turned me parallel to the ravine when I hit a small lemon tree at the top of the driveway on the ravine side.

I tried to open the door, but it was hard because of the angle of the car, so I looked at my brother and yelled, "Help me, you idiot!" He and his friend just stood there in shock. At that moment, the car slowly started to roll again toward the ravine, slamming the door on me and knocking me back to the driver's side door with my face plastered against the window. I started screaming as I was rolling into the ravine.

The car rolled two full times, and as it did I rolled onto the roof then into the back seat, then back on the roof and back into the front seat as glass was breaking all around me. The noise of crumpling metal and breaking glass was deafening from inside the car, and then it slammed into a large boulder with such force, throwing me into the passenger side foothold.

The silence was almost as deafening as the noise of the crash. My heart was pounding and my head hurt, and I felt heat coming from the car. As I regained my senses, I investigated the backseat and got chills as I realized the roof had been crushed down toward the back seat, where I was thrown for a moment as the car rolled over. I was able to push out the passenger door and crawl out onto the ice plant. I was out of breath and shaking and had a hard time standing up.

As I looked at myself for injuries, I saw no blood, but I felt a stinging sensation all over my body. I then realized that because I was in shorts with no shirt, I was covered with little slivers of glass stuck in my skin. I remember standing there shaking, and then I looked up and saw my brother, who said, "You are in so much trouble when Dad finds out." He then disappeared. I just stood there for a few minutes when suddenly my mother and stepfather appeared on the top edge of the ravine. My mom looked so worried yet relieved. My stepdad just stood there with his jaw clenched and then blurted out, "What the hell have you done to my car?" I knew I was in a lot of trouble, but as I started to climb the bank I blurted out, "Don't yell at me—I almost got killed."

As I reached the top of the ravine, my mother grabbed my hand, took me inside, and spent what felt like hours picking out the slivers of broken glass from my body with tweezers. Each removal brought a tiny speck of blood. I felt like a wounded soldier who had just survived a battle.

Now I am sure my mom was talking to me—I saw her lips move—but I don't remember a word that was said. I just kept thinking about how I almost died and that it was my brother's fault for pushing me over the bank.

My stepdad never said another word about it to me; it was so unlike him, but I was grateful. My parents had to have a crane come and lift that car out of the ravine and scrap it for metal.

Over the years, what was once a scary, expensive, and miraculous experience has become a funny story we relive and probably embellish every time we tell it. But I did learn some important lessons from that experience later in my life as I mentally relive that experience. Most important for me was how kind the Lord was in protecting me on so many levels that day from death and serious injury when I probably didn't deserve it. He truly is merciful and patient.

Upon further reflection, the interesting thing to me is that the car had all the necessary components to allow it to run safely and efficiently when it was turned on and powered by the engine. All that was required was regular maintenance and proper application of running the car in a safe and responsible manner. When run correctly, that car was a blessing to our family. However, that car was never intended to be driven without power, or by an unlawful and careless person like me. Although the car had power steering and power brakes, they could not provide the power required for me or anyone else to drive that car safely on any level when not turned on. There are so many correlations between a car and life.

We live in a world with great technology and advances that are amazing and can powerfully bless our lives. We have access to tools and resources that give us power to do incredible things very quickly and with great ease and comfort. Our world today can make us feel empowered to accomplish incredible things while saving time and effort in doing so. Yet if we are not careful, they can cause problems that flow from the very reason we love them.

Our lives are much like the car: we have all the right spiritual components to power our lives effectively and safely with regular maintenance and correct application of gospel principles in our lives. Too often, we try to do things on our own under the false idea that we are capable, when some things require power we cannot create or even access without correct application of principles that bring power into play.

It is true that God's power is available to everyone—the ability to steer through life safely and the power to brake when sin or danger appears. Further, the power to slow down and merge with caution in situations that arise that require special attention. When we try to travel through life quickly on our own without God's power, simply because we feel we have the faculties and abilities to do so, it can put us in dangerous situations that may then require God's benevolence to save us from further danger, injury, or even death. This goes beyond just physical injuries and includes emotional, psychological, and spiritual possibilities. Everything has a price for its use, and at times the price can cost us more than just regular maintenance or occasional fixing. Living with spiritual power can help us avoid the temporal and spiritual ravines in our lives.

Ponder this question from your own perspective: what is more critical in helping a car run properly? The keys, the engine, the steering wheel, the wheels, or the brakes? You could make a case for all these things individually. However, we must look at the car in its totality to understand the importance of all those components.

I once heard of an analogy that used the car to represent priesthood power. The car, when running properly, can bless more than the driver; it can allow others to travel safely in it. Priesthood power when functioning properly can bless everyone: the individual exercising the priesthood and many others affected by its power. Its true value, though, is dependent upon many factors. Those who exercise the priesthood and those who benefit from it have specific responsibilities to make sure it functions at full power. Like the car, there are important components needed to make it run properly and safely for everyone concerned. Perhaps a simple comparison helps us visualize the relationship of these power parts.

- Key = priesthood authority
- Engine = priesthood power unlocked by personal worthiness
- Steering wheel = how priesthood power is used under the direction of the Spirit
- Wheels = moving in the right direction; being bold enough to command when inspired to do so
- Brakes = stopping or holding back; being meek enough to follow the Spirit's direction over our own desires.

No one component is more important than any other component; they must work together for the car or the priesthood to move us in the direction we need to go safely. However, there is an added component here that is also critical. The car works best when driven by one who has been tested and who is responsible enough to drive the car properly. This is analogous to a covenant-keeping person whose faith has been tested, and they have been proven worthy to use the priesthood appropriately or to be blessed and empowered by it.

When we are not prepared, not knowledgeable in the things of God, and when we try to use or access power in our lives for selfish or unrealistic reasons, we will not have the power necessary to keep us safe.

Keeping our covenants is critical. Keeping our covenants of salvation, our baptismal covenants, prepares us to enter covenants of exaltation found in the temple. Covenants coupled with obedience will drive us to our ultimate destination of eternal life. I love the following scripture that clarifies our priesthood-car analogy and our part in making sure it is working properly:

> Therefore, let every man stand in his own office, and labor in his own calling; and let not the head say unto the feet it hath no need of the feet; for without the feet how shall the body be able to stand?
>
> Also the body hath need of every member, that all may be edified together, that the system may be kept perfect. (D&C 84:109–110)

We must learn our role as a component of the gospel of Jesus Christ so we can function properly in our quest to travel safely in our journey here. I readily acknowledge that Heavenly Father is the master engineer, and through our personal agency we can turn the driving over to Him, remembering that man does not drive the priesthood. The Lord's counsel is clear:

> Behold, there are many called, but few are chosen. And why are they not chosen?
>
> Because their hearts are set so much upon the things of this world, and aspire to the honors of men, that they do not learn this one lesson—
>
> That the rights of the priesthood are inseparably connected with the powers of heaven, and that the powers of heaven cannot be controlled nor handled only upon the principles of righteousness.
>
> That they may be conferred upon us, it is true; but when we undertake to cover our sins, or to gratify our pride, our vain ambition, or to exercise control or dominion or compulsion upon the souls of the children of men, in any degree of unrighteousness, behold, the heavens withdraw themselves; the Spirit of the Lord is grieved; and when it is withdrawn, Amen to the priesthood or the authority of that man. (D&C 121:34–37)

Heavenly Father knows our divine potential and how to get us back home to His presence. He has provided through His Son priesthood power to bless the lives of His children here and on the other side of the veil. When we recognize where that power comes from and how to turn it on by keeping our covenants, we can drive safely as individuals and families through the trials of life back home to our heavenly parents.

Who is in the car, who is driving the car, and how it is being used means everything to the safety of the passengers and others on the highways of mortality.

Principle to Live By

Learn to access God's priesthood power by keeping our covenants and be blessed by it, and then bless the lives of others in our journey through mortality toward a heavenly home.

23

Running My Sister Over with a Bike

Don't taunt our circumstances

I don't honestly remember how old I was; I only know I was able to ride a bike well. My sister Nannette is three years younger than me, and we were both young and obnoxious enough to cause an accident.

We lived in an area and neighborhood where there were lots of kids our age. It was great because there was always something going on in the neighborhood, and when there wasn't, we could fall back on the old trusted entertainment of bike riding around the block. The sidewalk was flat and wide, so we did not have to ride in the street. Traffic back then was never a problem, and people drove slowly enough that we never felt uneasy about riding around the neighborhood alone, either in the street on the sidewalk.

One afternoon, I was just enjoying riding back and forth on our street, sometimes swerving onto the sidewalk when a driveway presented itself, getting some air off the little inclines of the opening back onto the sidewalk. I remember my legs weren't strong enough to generate speed while sitting down, so I would pedal standing up and swaying side to side as I pushed my weight down on each peddle to increase speed.

I was just riding with no real purpose in mind other than the thrill of generating speed and occasionally slamming on the pedal brakes, sliding to the side to lay down some rubber on the sidewalk. That allowed me later to point out to my buddies or a cute girl how cool I was and the status of my bike-riding abilities.

Anyway, as I was riding back toward my house, I saw my little sister standing in the middle of the sidewalk, leaning forward with her hands on her hips, swaying behind back and forth with a defiant look on her face. I yelled, "Get out of the way," but she just stood there in that same position, taunting me, and so I yelled again, "You better get out of the way, or I will run over you!" My threat had no effect upon her at all; she thought that at the last moment I would turn onto the lawn and go around her. What she didn't know was my commitment level to staying on course and running her over if she did not move. I just believed she would jump out of the way at the very last moment and say something sarcastic as I passed.

As I got closer, I started cranking out the speed and yelled one last time with emphasis to get out of the way. Suddenly, I was upon her, and she never moved. I ran right into her, and she fell backward, flat on her back, and I ran right up the center of her body and over her face with ease.

As I finished running her over and experienced the rush of that Evel Knievel–like accomplishment, I looked back as I kept pedaling and saw Nannette lying flat on the sidewalk screaming, so I just kept on going. I never broke stride and rode around the corner and kept on going around the block, thinking I was going to be in so much trouble, knowing Nan would blame the whole incident on me.

As I made it around the block and to the end of our street, I stopped and looked to see what was going on in front of our house. Nan was not on the sidewalk, and I assumed she was inside getting medical attention for her wounds. I just stood there with my bike, waiting for my mother to come out calling me by my full name without spaces—WINNDONALDLEERALEIGH—verifying my suspicion that I was in deep trouble. But she never came out, and I never heard that name. I was confused but kind of relieved and then quickly became even more fearful of what would happen when I went home.

I finally started the slow ride home, wondering what was going to happen to me.

The whole incident happened so fast, and it wasn't very long before I was back in front of my house to see my sister sitting on the front porch, waiting for me. I swear, and so will my brother, she was wrapped up like a mummy. I am not kidding, her whole body was wrapped, and I thought to myself, there is no way my mom had enough time to do that. But my sister did not seem to have any serious injuries or wounds—no blood, just some discoloration from my tires running over her face. It was amazing yet odd. Nan just said, "You're in trouble with Mom." I do remember I suffered some kind of restriction involving my bike and frequent accusations from my sister that it was my fault. But I most clearly remember the accident, and I do feel bad about it now, even as I am laughing while writing this.

From this experience I learned not to taunt circumstances. Both my sister and I taunted one another into the collision. I was older and should have known better and avoided the accident altogether, waiting for some future moment to pull a dirty trick on her to get even. Often, when we admit some part in an adverse outcome, we still try to justify ourselves in some way. What I am talking about is pride. Pride can manifest itself in many ways: comparison, envy, judgment, puffy self-esteem, enmity, withholding affection, and so much more. Pride always causes a collision between man and God, one another, doctrines, ideals, laws, and so forth.

Concerning where pride can begin, there is a fascinating scripture in the Book of Mormon. Notice in the following verses where pride began, what caused it, and how it was manifested outwardly.

> And it came to pass in the eighth year of the reign of the judges, that the people of the church began to wax proud, because of

> their exceeding riches, and their fine silks, and their fine-twined linen, and because of their many flocks and herds, and their gold and their silver, and all manner of precious things, which they had obtained by their industry; and in all these things were they lifted up in the pride of their eyes, for they began to wear very costly apparel.
>
> Now this was the cause of much affliction to Alma, yea, and to many of the people whom Alma had consecrated to be teachers, and priests, and elders over the church; yea, many of them were sorely grieved for the wickedness which they saw had begun to be among their people.
>
> For they saw and beheld with great sorrow that the people of the church began to be lifted up in the pride of their eyes, and to set their hearts upon riches and upon the vain things of the world, that they began to be scornful, one towards another, and they began to persecute those that did not believe according to their own will and pleasure.
>
> And thus, in this eighth year of the reign of the judges, there began to be great contentions among the people of the church; yea, there were envyings, and strife, and malice, and persecutions, and pride, even to exceed the pride of those who did not belong to the church of God. (Alma 4:6–9)

Because of worldly stuff and weak reasoning, pride manifested itself in the believers of Christ. Followers of God and Christ are not precluded from becoming prideful, and where it can begin is insightful: "pride in their eyes." What we look at and how we process it determines the quality of the heart. If we are focused on the world, then we will be influenced by its visually impairing attributes. Now there is certainly nothing wrong with success and our pursuit of it to better our lives and the lives of those we have influence over. But if we are simply affected by what we see before us and we fix upon it, if it is not for our betterment, then we will become what we dislike most in others and what we consider to be prideful.

In my experience with my sister, we were too prideful to move and to give in. In life, we are taunted by things that capture our attention, emotions, passions, and appetites. We are also tempted by others who come across as being in opposition to us, or often as a pretended ally to get us to give in and comply. What we focus on, how we internalize what it means to us, can elevate or destroy us.

So what is a potential remedy? Again, the Book of Mormon is insightful. The Lord understanding the tendencies of the natural man and woman establishes the doctrine for us all:

> Lay not up for yourselves treasures upon earth, where moth and rust doth corrupt, and thieves break through and steal;
>
> But lay up for yourselves treasures in heaven, where neither moth nor rust doth corrupt, and where thieves do not break through nor steal.
>
> For where your treasure is, there will your heart be also.
>
> The light of the body is the eye; if, therefore, thine eye be single, thy whole body shall be full of light.
>
> But if thine eye be evil, thy whole body shall be full of darkness. If, therefore, the light that is in thee be darkness, how great is that darkness! (3 Nephi 13:19–23)

Learning to focus our eyes, physically and spiritually, on things that bring light into our lives helps us to avoid pride that is developed by looking at worldliness and darkness and then internalizing it. I believe that is why we are invited by the Lord to feast upon His word daily. Daily scripture study ensures that our eyes are focused for even a short time every day on light, which will help us not to dwell or focus on the darkness so prevalent and appealing in our daily walk. Eyes filled with light avoid the prideful taunting toward others and our circumstances.

Principle to Live By

Learn to process carefully what we see, focusing daily on light-giving activities to avoid becoming prideful and colliding with God's will, others, and our circumstances.

24

The Cruise Ship, Snap Bands, and Ginger Pills

Choosing the right remedies in life

Something you should know about me is that I get seasick. I also get car sick. In fact, I get motion sickness in general, and especially if I am thrown around quickly by some crazy mind-bending ride that turns me upside down or sideways.

As a teenager, we had a thirty-foot Erickson sailboat called "Happiness Is." The trouble was it really wasn't happiness for some of us non-sailors in the family. My stepfather was a very accomplished sailor and had experienced the Trans Pack race sailing to Hawaii. He grew up on the beach sailing, and he loved it so much he assumed we all would as well. We did not!

It seemed like every weekend we would leave our slip in the harbor and sail all day long. Our mouths would start to water with a bad bitter taste of acid from our stomachs, and we just knew it would not be long before we were on the "heave" side, chumming the water. It was a stinking nightmare, and the worst part of it was that once we finally got off the boat, we still felt nauseous for hours after.

My poor mom tried every remedy she could think of, or hear of, to make our weekend trips bearable. We finally found that lemon juice worked somewhat, along with eating some saltine crackers.

Unfortunately, we did not enjoy the regular all-day weekend trips enough, though, so eventually my stepfather sold the boat.

Don't get me wrong—I love the ocean; I'm just not big on sailing, so I was hesitant when my brother-in-law and his family invited our family to go on a cruise with them. I knew that experienced cruisers still got sick during big storms on the ocean but figured maybe I had outgrown my youthful seasickness. These cruise lines are so big, so I thought the chances of me getting sick were slim, and I decided to give it a go. However, after talking to our experienced family cruisers, they said I still needed to take something with me to be prepared when we would encounter rough seas.

When I was talking to my mother about our upcoming cruise, she suggested using pressure wrist bands and ginger pills. Some of you may be wondering why I didn't just take some Dramamine for the trip. That is an excellent question—that I cannot answer. My excuse was that I had never been on a cruise before and didn't know any better, and that turned out to be a lame excuse.

Some of you are also wondering what a pressure wristband is. It is something you can buy at a pharmacy as a remedy, so I figured it must work, especially if my mom suggested it. The ginger pills—I have no idea what that is supposed to do, but again it was a motherly suggestion, so I bought into the idea that it would work. I bought those technological marvels and thought I was ready to go. The wristband is nothing more than a sweatband. They were performance-enhancing equipment, simple but effective. My sweatbands had special technology—a little plastic protrusion on the inside of the band to press against the inside of the wrist, putting pressure on something that is supposed to control nausea.

The ginger pills supposedly contain some sort of ingredient to help calm the stomach juices and to help you not throw up. And of course, that is the most important thing while on a cruise—don't throw up, at all costs. The pills themselves were huge, and you couldn't swallow them, so they had to be chewed up so that they got to the stomach immediately and would work quickly. However, I found out later they were so nasty-tasting that chewing them would make you sick. I guess I was doomed to get sick one way or the other.

Except for telling my wife, I didn't reveal my remedies to anyone until we got on the ship and were under way. Unfortunately, that first night was rough, and I was already feeling gassy and had to lay down in our cabin and close my eyes to try and control the nausea. The storm was so bad that all activities on the boat were shut down and everyone had to go to their cabins; I soon found out everyone else was struggling as well.

I started snapping a wristband so the pain would help distract me from the nausea. Not only did it not work, but it also caused a deep indent in my wrist and made it red and tender. Now I turned to the ginger pills, which were my back-up plan; certainly they would work, right? Why would my mom suggest something that would not work? So, taking courage, I chowed down two of those ginger pills quickly and waited for my stomach to calm down as I continued snapping away on my two wristbands. Soon I was rolling back and forth, moaning from the now amplified nausea raging in my body.

I realized all too late that my remedies were voodoo, and the only effect it was having was to enhance my sickness to a level I had not experienced before or even since. I WAS NOT ENJOYING THIS TRIP!

For the next four days, I suffered through this pattern of snapping and gingering until I gave up and just went outside for some fresh air. Funny thing, as I made it up to the main deck without retching in front of everyone, I felt better almost immediately. It was wonderful, and as I walked around outside on the deck, feeling the cool breeze on my face, my stomach started to calm down. I even ate a little something and got some strength back. As I started to pay attention to my surroundings, I discovered there was free all-you-could-eat everything and a variety of delights that would make anyone happy. Unfortunately, I had missed all of that for most of our trip because I traded real remedies for strange magic. What an idiot I was, yet I cannot blame my mother or anyone else.

For years after, and to this day, my brother-in-law and his family make fun of me for my strange remedies. I now know I should have used the famous cruising patch worn behind the ear, or the time-tested drug Dramamine, or several other available remedies that are proven to work. But no, I chose the snapper and ginger pills.

What is the lesson here? For me it is all about finding and applying the right remedy for a specific situation. There are a variety of challenges and circumstances we face in life, so there are a variety of remedies we can use in specific situations. From a spiritual perspective, there are principles we can apply to very specific situations, and some that have a very general and broad application. The challenge is learning how to apply the right principle in the right way for the maximum outcome or blessing.

We know not all circumstances are equal, so not all principles are equal. But correct application is the remedy and the key to success. Just applying a principle in our own way that is not in harmony with the Lord's will is of no value, just like my wristband and the ginger pills.

Now let me clarify something—the wristband and ginger pills still may be the right remedy for someone else under the right circumstances. Let me explain:

Truth exists independent of all things, and as wiser men have taught, all divine truth is packaged in principles for practical application in our lives in a variety of circumstances. For example, the statement that God hears and answers prayers is a true doctrinal statement, whether anyone believes it or not. One of many principles attached to that doctrine would be prayer. The application is simple in this situation: one must pray to come to a knowledge that God hears and answers prayers. Although this principle is specific, the application varies. And when an individual prays and that prayer is answered, then that doctrine comes alive in their life, and their relationship with God changes because they now know that He truly does hear and answer prayers.

Application is the key to accessing the power of doctrines and attending principles. In this example of prayer, application of that one principle may be different for every individual. One person may need to just start praying daily, another may need to pray more sincerely, others using different language or praying longer, still another with greater faith, or perhaps some may need to stay on their knees after prayer and listen for answers. The list of applications can go on and on for just that one principle. It is the application that is critical and is like a remedy for our specific challenges or needs in life.

Unfortunately, there are times when we may apply a principle in a way that is not the way the Lord has prescribed for an optimal result. We may apply a principle in a way that is comfortable or convenient for us but does not access the promised blessings and intended effect God desires for us and the result we desire for ourselves. The challenge is to find the correct application for our circumstances, and this requires that we are influenced by the Spirit and not by our own desires.

I have learned a great principle that applies to all people. Whenever we read or listen to counsel and instruction, we should do so for its intended application, never for preference or exception. The Lord through the Spirit must be the one who makes an exception for the application of true principles. We find this principle in the scriptures:

> Trust in the Lord with all thine heart; and lean not unto thine own understanding.
>
> In all thy ways acknowledge him, and he shall direct thy paths. (Proverbs 3:5–6)

Inherent in the idea that we cannot rely upon our own understanding or interpretation is the companion principle of wisdom:

> Wisdom is the principal thing; therefore get wisdom: and with all thy getting get understanding. (Proverbs 4:7)

Wisdom is not based upon a quantity of knowledge but rather the quality of knowledge that allows a person to apply acquired knowledge wisely. A wise individual will seek the Lord's help in the application of the knowledge and understanding required to do the right thing. We find a great example of this in the Book of Mormon as Nephi is teaching his brothers:

> Wherefore, now after I have spoken these words, if ye cannot understand them it will be because ye ask not, neither do ye knock; wherefore, ye are not brought into the light, but must perish in the dark. (2 Nephi 32:4)

Correct application of truth requires asking for understanding and direction. We need to more patiently seek for the influence of the Spirit to teach us what is expedient for us. Then, when we pray for our desires, it will be right and our application will be the correct one because it is according to the will of the Lord. Application, like remedies, can mean everything in understanding and facing our challenges in life. We must make sure the remedy matches the moment.

Principle to Live By

When we invite the Spirit to help us know how to apply a principle of truth correctly, it will bless us in the most appropriate way for our unique needs and circumstances.

25

Left Hanging on a Cliff

Climb in the right direction with the right help

I grew up around empty lots and hillsides to explore, climb, and generally have fun on. Near our home there was an interesting couple of vacant lots on the hillside. One was nearly on the same level as our home, and the other was thirty feet below this upper lot. The upper lot also had a decomposed granite cliff wall about ten to twelve feet high from its floor up to the brush-covered hill.

One day my brother and I were playing around on the upper lot when I got an idea to climb the granite cliff to the brush-covered hill above. No real reason; I was a kid who just saw a cliff and thought I could climb it.

I had my brother stand below as I began my climb to tell me where I could put my feet or hands as I climbed. When you are clinging to the wall of a cliff, you don't have the needed perspective, and an inexperienced climber like a kid has enough fear in them to keep them plastered to the wall with very little movement going on. Because I just looked straight ahead, I lost perspective of my surroundings.

My brother would try to tell me places I could grab or a place I could rest my foot on, but because my head was turned to the left side and I was too afraid to move my head back and forth to survey the cliff, I just moved my eyes so that my movements did not cause me to lose my balance.

I did not know it at the time, but because I was only looking to left side with my cheek touching the cliff, I was not just moving upward, but I was naturally also moving to the right as I was climbing. I thought I was higher than I was because I was moving in two directions, which made it feel like I had been climbing a long time without reaching the top. Now I was climbing out of fear and felt that if I did not hurry I was going to lose my strength and fall backward onto my back and head, leaving me crippled or dead.

Finally, without moving my head much, I could strain my eyes upward to see I was just a few feet from the top, and I thought for a moment I was going to make it. If I could just get close enough to reach up and grab one of the sagebrush limbs, I could pull myself up the rest of the way. I had a guarded grin on my face when, for the first time, I looked down to see where I was in relation to my brother. As I looked, I noticed that because I was climbing at a right angle upward, I was now over the lower lot, so the fall was about thirty feet, not ten feet. I panicked and started to whimper a little as my breathing became rapid and heavy with fear. Now I was sure I was going to die.

My thoughts started racing, and I panicked about what to do. It was hard to think because my thoughts of death and injury were so vivid in my mind, and I thought there was no way out. How could I possibly continue to climb upward, knowing I was over a much higher and more dangerous drop? So I just froze. As I hung there, my brother said he would run home and get someone to come help. I told him not to do that, fearing I would get in trouble for even being in that dangerous position.

As I clung to that cliff wall, I suddenly had an idea, and I told Mike to go home and get the long bamboo stick in the garage and then climb up to the hill above me and pull me up. What a dumb idea! First of all, my little brother would have trouble just climbing the hill through thick sagebrush to get above me, and secondly, he wasn't strong enough to pull me up to the top. I'm sure I would have pulled him over the cliff as well, but that reasoning came long after the incident, and at that moment I just needed help. So I told him to hurry.

My brother yelled okay, and I heard him running away; I did not dare to try to turn my head to watch him head home, so I just clung to the granite wall and felt some relief as I thought I was going to get off the cliff safely. It was hard waiting and not being able to see him at a distance running back to help me. I just tried to listen for his running feet and hoped it would not be long before I heard him yelling, "I'm coming!"

I did not hear that. In fact, what must have been five to ten minutes later—I could not accurately tell—what I heard was a bunch of kids running up the hill laughing and screaming. I thought to myself, *Mike got help from our friends, and they are on their way to the rescue.* However, the impending rescue never came, and a few minutes later I heard the group of kids now running down the hill yelling and screaming, so I got the courage to turn my head, and what I saw was my brother bring up the rear of a group of four to five neighbor kids having a good time. Apparently, my brother got side-tracked on the way home with the neighborhood kids playing, and so he thought he would join in.

You cannot be serious! I thought. *My life is hanging in the balance and my brother is playing tag.* I got so mad and thought to myself, *Just wait until I get hold of him.* Without thinking, I just started climbing upward until I got hold of a bush and yanked myself up on top of the cliff. It caused some pain, but the adrenaline pushed me upward.

When I got to the top, I stopped to check myself out, and although I was scratched up and my fingers and nails were bruised and a little bloodied up, I was off the cliff and safe, and that was all that mattered. I did have some trouble wading through the sagebrush back to the road. It is funny how we are so happy to be in a safe place after being bruised and wounded by an experience, when in fact we often put ourselves in an unsafe situation. How ironic that we often start out in safety but then do something to put ourselves at risk.

For our purposes, and from my perspective, there is also a lesson here on making sure when we are climbing in life to improve ourselves or our circumstances that we are climbing the right cliff with the right help, and certainly in the right direction. If we are not mindful of our abilities, those we rely upon, and we just start climbing without purpose, preparation, commitment, and focused attention, we can end up in a tough situation that may require us to get ourselves back to safety. There are those ugly consequences again.

I do believe the Lord will always be willing to help us when we make honest mistakes. However, it may take a while and require great effort and time on our part because we put ourselves in those circumstances in the first place. A wise man once said you cannot talk yourself out of behavior you lived yourself into. I believe this is true. Sometimes the Lord requires us to live ourselves out of our behavior. Or in other words, He requires us to climb upward without looking back and without lingering in fear. So what do the scriptures have to say about climbing and direction?

> And Jesus entered and passed through Jericho.
>
> And, behold, there was a man named Zacchæus, which was the chief among the publicans, and he was rich.
>
> And he sought to see Jesus who he was; and could not for the press, because he was little of stature.
>
> And he ran before, and climbed up into a sycamore tree to see him: for he was to pass that way.
>
> Verily, verily, I say unto you, He that entereth not by the door into the sheepfold, but climbeth up some other way, the same is a thief and a robber. (John 10:1–5)

The purpose and direction of our climb determines how the Lord characterizes us. In this instance, someone is climbing up to see the Lord, and a better perspective is required. In my experience, I was not climbing with a purpose other than to climb. I did not consider why or how or what I would do when I got there. Sometimes in life, we are like children just doing things because we want to, with no real forethought or purpose in mind. Others climb purposefully as a thief, robbing themselves of spirituality and real satisfaction. We would do well to ask ourselves, *Are we climbing to gain a clearer perspective of the Savior, or are we just climbing to appease our own selfish desires?* In our consideration of why we climb, commitment becomes a key element.

> And whosoever doth not bear his cross, and come after me, cannot be my disciple.
>
> For which of you, intending to build a tower, sitteth not down first, and counteth the cost, whether he have sufficient to finish it?
>
> Lest haply, after he hath laid the foundation, and is not able to finish it, all that behold it begin to mock him,
>
> Saying, This man began to build, and was not able to finish. (Luke 14:28–30)

Whether we are building something or climbing something, there must be commitment. We must consider the cost and be willing and able to finish. Unlike me—I did not consider the potential cost of climbing, that I could get tired, injured, or worse. And when things got tough because I climbed in the wrong direction, I wanted to quit and turned in desperation to someone who was not capable of helping me. A natural consequence of not counting the cost is that when things don't go well, we tend to blame others. I placed blame on my brother, who had nothing to do with my problem. Counting the cost of what we undertake to do will largely determine the outcome. So what about effort?

> Come, my brethren, every one that thirsteth, come ye to the waters; and he that hath no money, come buy and eat; yea, come buy wine and milk without money and without price.
>
> Wherefore, do not spend money for that which is of no worth, nor your labor for that which cannot satisfy. Hearken diligently unto me, and remember the words which I have spoken; and

> come unto the Holy One of Israel, and feast upon that which perisheth not, neither can be corrupted, and let your soul delight in fatness. (2 Nephi 9:50–51)

We must labor for things that truly satisfy, and here it is described as "fatness." Fatness is a state of being and a quality of being. It's the state and quality of satisfaction when it saturates the soul. It is laboring for things with reason that really matter most. Many today labor for the wrong things and with hollow and meaningless reasons. They are climbing in the wrong direction, focused on the wrong kind of fatness—a worldly fatness that is wasteful in nature and accumulates around the belly of selfishness. This is not satisfying; it is an uncontrolled appetite of emotion or passion. The Lord's "fatness" is a fullness of joy and happiness reserved for followers of righteousness. A follower of righteousness labors with focus. Notice the Lord's idea of focus and what it can lead to:

> And if your eye be single to my glory, your whole bodies shall be filled with light, and there shall be no darkness in you; and that body which is filled with light comprehendeth all things.
>
> Therefore, sanctify yourselves that your minds become single to God, and the days will come that you shall see him; for he will unveil his face unto you, and it shall be in his own time, and in his own way, and according to his own will. (D&C 88:67–68)

As we contemplate our efforts and desires to climb upward spiritually, we need to be focused on those things that lead us to safety and not further peril. We need to listen and rely upon the right people who can help guide us and who are strong enough to help us when we are weak from climbing. Of course, the Savior is the ultimate help, strength, and example.

When our eyes and minds are single and focused on the Lord, we can more easily comprehend the footholds and safest ascent of life to where we desire to be. We will always be climbing in the right direction for the right reason, and when we become tired or unsure, He will always be there to give guidance, direction, encouragement, and strength to enable us to continue until we reach the safety of His presence. Climb, but climb in the right direction with focus and for the right reasons.

Principle to Live By

Learn to avoid dangerous ground, and focus on the Savior as we climb in life. Know and understand the cost of discipleship, and be willing to labor until we reach safer ground.

26

A Temple Dedication

Assuming the foot of the table

When the San Diego Temple was under construction, I was privileged to serve as the stake mission president. This was my favorite calling for several reasons, one obviously being because of our involvement in preparing for the temple open house prior to its dedication. And certainly because of the missionary work that would flow from our involvement. A more personal reason was because, for a time, my brother served as one of my counselors. This is a calling that no longer exists in the church, so it was unique and special to me. It was especially sweet to be part of the preparations for the open house, for the public to go through and learn more about temple work itself.

One of my friends happened to be one of the lead supervisors for the construction of the temple, and on several occasions, he took my wife and I on a tour of the work as it was progressing. It was a special time for everyone in San Diego who understood the significance of what was happening and the blessings that would be poured out upon the community.

During this time, there were many miraculous things happening, and I want to share one as it related to my calling. While in the beginning of the construction of the temple, I needed to call another counselor in the mission presidency to serve with me. I did not take this lightly and spent much time in prayer and consideration of all the men who were capable to serve. I went through the stake directory, asked the opinion and suggestions of people I respected, along with seeking inspiration from the Lord. I got nothing. I had been making a list of individuals but could not get an answer, and it troubled me. This went on for several months, and I started to question my own ability to receive inspiration.

Finally, I told Heavenly Father, *This is Your Son's work, and I am not getting any direction. I need a name now.* Surprisingly, a name popped into my head that I did not recognize, so I got excited and went to the stake directory looking for this specific name but could not find it. I started to ask stake leaders if they knew this individual, and found no one had heard of this person. Again, I was stunned and frustrated; this was an important time in the work, and I needed an experienced counselor to serve.

One Sunday, weeks after receiving the name, I was at our ward building for some church meetings and I saw one of our high councilors. He looked like he was in a hurry to take care of some business, but I stopped him and quickly passed the name by him. He initially responded that he did not know the man nor recognize the name. As he was leaving, he suddenly stopped halfway down the hallway and turned around, and as he approached me he opened his briefcase to look at a form that had the name of a new member who had just moved in the stake. In fact, it was the individual he was going to meet with and extend to him a calling. Something in the name rang a bell with this priesthood leader, and as he examined the paper and the name, it was the same surname that popped into my head weeks earlier, but the man happened to go by his middle name. This was the man!

The priesthood leader told me that this man had been living in Japan because he was in the military and was just transferred to the States a couple of weeks earlier, so he was not on any records or known by anyone when I received his name. The amazing thing was that he was serving as the stake mission president in Japan at the time I received his name, weeks before he ever arrived in the States. This man was called and was such a blessing to the work and our preparations for the temple open house and the missionary work that followed. This was just one of many miraculous things to happen in the work while the temple was being constructed.

I tell you this so that you might more fully understand how I felt about my calling and the important work attending our responsibilities at this time. I knew it was Spirit-driven, and as completion neared there was a lot of excitement and anticipation of the open house and dedication of our temple. We did not need to travel three to four hours one way to the Los Angeles Temple any longer. We now had a temple in our own backyard, and we could not wait for its completion and the attending celebrations that would take place.

As the open house details were rolling out with specific assignments, the dates set and preparations underway, there was a lot of talk about the dedicatory sessions that would follow.

When specific details were announced, dates, times, and people, the conversations turned to who would be invited to be in the celestial room with the visiting authorities. I heard some assume that because of their callings they would be privileged to be in that special room with all the dignitaries. Unfortunately, for a time I too started to assume that because of my calling and responsibilities with the open house preparations that I would receive a special ticket to this event. Surely I deserved it.

Looking back, I am embarrassed that I ever got caught up in that kind of aspiring speculation, but I did. However, I quickly course corrected after reading the scriptures one day and happened upon Mark chapter 14. This is what I read:

> And he put forth a parable to those which were bidden, when he marked how they chose out the chief rooms; saying unto them,
>
> When thou art bidden of any man to a wedding, sit not down in the highest room; lest a more honourable man than thou be bidden of him;

> And he that bade thee and him come and say to thee, Give this man place; and thou begin with shame to take the lowest room.
>
> But when thou art bidden, go and sit down in the lowest room; that when he that bade thee cometh, he may say unto thee, Friend, go up higher: then shalt thou have worship in the presence of them that sit at meat with thee.
>
> For whosoever exalteth himself shall be abased; and he that humbleth himself shall be exalted. (Luke 14:7–11)

My perspective changed immediately, and I had to repent and humble myself before the Lord and ask His forgiveness for being so prideful as to assume I should sit in the highest room. I started to pray that my wife and I would just be able to be in the temple during one of the sessions. I did not care if we had to sit in the kitchen or laundry room and listen to it on the speaker system. I just wanted to be in that special house and feel the Spirit of that sacred event.

Weeks passed, and I struggled to control my thoughts and feelings but felt good about myself and the privilege it was to be part of that special work. I did not hone in on the conversations of others any longer, as it did not matter to me anymore. Then, a few days before the scheduled dedication, I was in our chapel and saw the stake president down the hall looking around as if he needed to find someone. He locked eyes with me and extended his hand and beckoned me with his finger to come to him. He seemed anxious, and so I walked toward him quickly, not knowing why he wanted to meet with me. He took me into an empty classroom and asked if I had any grown children, and I said no, that it was just me and my wife at home. He then took two tickets out of his coat pocket and said, "I felt impressed to hold onto these tickets until I was inspired as to who I should give them to. When I saw you, Winn, the Spirit whispered to me that they were for you and your wife."

I was overcome with emotion. What a sweet tender mercy the Lord had extended to me and my wife for humbling myself before Him and for acknowledging my weakness to Him. I do know and can testify with authenticity that if we will but strive to humble ourselves and always try to assume the lowest chambers or foot of the table in the Lord's work, on occasion He will invite us to the upper rooms and the head of the table.

My wife and I were privileged to be seated in the celestial room within a few feet of President Thomas S. Monson, who was giving the dedicatory prayer for President Hinckley during that session. A funny side note is that the day before, my wife had a dream where she saw President Monson in the celestial room in place of the prophet President Hinckley, who could not attend at the last moment. She told me this and I did not believe her, but when we got there and I found out she was right, I just knew it was going to be a special experience.

We both had very personal and profound experiences in the temple that day. I know that we would not have had that experience had I not humbled myself before the Lord. I can't imagine almost causing my wife to have sacrificed such a personal experience in the temple because I entertained selfish desires for myself.

I am grateful for the Lord's example and for His patience and kindness in my own struggles in life. But at times, when we get it right, I am in awe of how He honors us for our righteous desires to be more like Him and a little less like ourselves. If we cleanse our temple, the Lord will bless us in His temple in personal and unique ways.

Principle to Live By

When we strive to humble ourselves before the Lord and always assume the foot of the table in His work, the Lord at times will invite us in a personal way to sit at the head of His table and enjoy His presence in unique ways.

27

Dane and a Volleyball Championship Game

Honor the Lord and He will honor you

My son Dane is a good athlete. He was a good basketball player, very tenacious and always hustling. But he was a great volleyball player. He was touted as one of the five best volleyball players in Santa Clarita and was all-league in a place where volleyball is huge. Valencia High School has for many years been one of the top schools in the nation, sending many players on full-ride scholarships to programs like UCLA and Long Beach University, perennial national championship programs.

After my son graduated from high school, we moved from Los Angeles back to San Diego, and then my son left on a two-year mission to Monterrey, Mexico. He had not played volleyball for two years but was interested in playing when he got home. Dane decided he would try to get back into school by going to a small college in San Diego and then try to transfer to BYU. So, I decided to contact the head volleyball coach and see if Dane could tryout as a walk-on athlete. He was excited when he saw Dane's stats and career in high school and welcomed him gladly when he came home from his mission.

Dane competed well with the other taller hitters on the team and got playing time. Soon, the coaches noticed Dane's soft hands and his ability to pass the ball very accurately, so they changed his position to libero, a designated passing and digging specialist on the team. His first year, he received the coach's award for his play and positive influence on the team.

Dane's second year, the team was getting attention for its players and potential to play for the state title. The team won the league and rolled through the playoffs, putting them in the state finals for the first time in the history of the school.

In preparation for the state championship, the coach called a Sunday practice, something that had not happened before in Dane's career. We were interested to see how Dane would respond and were proud of him when he told the coach that he could not come to practice on a Sunday because he attended church with his family. The coach did not take this well and told Dane if he did not show up he would not start and would not play. Dane talked to us about his situation and how frustrating it would be if he could not play in such an important game for himself, the program, and the college. Dane did not waver, however, and told the coach he would not attend the practice.

As we went to the state championship game, something interesting happened. Prior to the match, as the players gathered together as they usually did to psych themselves up with chants and cheers, they asked Dane to offer a prayer. There was a quiet, more focused feel this time, different from other pre-game rituals.

As the match began, things did not go well from the beginning, but Dane remained positive and was a cheerleader from the bench, encouraging everyone.

Dane's team got beaten badly the first two games, not even reaching twenty points in either game. It felt like it was going to be a quick sweep of us and we would look terrible in losing. Not a way you want to celebrate the school's first state championship experience.

Fortunately for us, there is always a break between the second and third games, giving the losing team a chance to regain composure and tighten up mistakes, and everyone was quiet and sullen about what was happening. As the teams returned for what we thought would be the final game, Dane was warming up behind the bench, and we all got guardedly excited because the coach was adamant that Dane would not play. But he did, because the assistant coaches petitioned for him to play.

As the team walked onto the court, there was a different feeling about the team; they were upbeat and excited. Their posture was different, and Dane had them energized. They swept the next two games easily, causing pandemonium in the venue. It was electric and now everyone, including the other team, felt that the momentum had turned—we were sure our team would take the fifth and deciding game. What a way to win a championship.

As the fifth game started, it turned quickly into our favor and at one point we were up eleven to seven with match point at fifteen. Then the rotation changed where the libero comes out and another hitter is placed in the rotation, and even though we should have had an advantage with an extra hitter, our guys suddenly could not pass the ball accurately, so the sets were not good and the hitters started making unforced hitting errors. We ultimately lost fifteen to thirteen, and it was all because of unforced errors.

It turned out that the assistant coaches had to convince the head coach to put Dane in the game, and he made all the difference on the bench and on the court. Dane was skilled, but he was also a good person, and that was felt by all his peers, parents, and coaches. Interestingly, at the season-ending banquet Dane again received the coach's award for being the most inspirational player on the team. His head coach said that he was the best young man he had ever coached in his career. I believe it was largely because Dane chose to honor God over a game.

I felt for a time how unfair it was that Dane was punished for honoring Heavenly Father, His son, and the Sabbath Day. Dane sacrificed a great deal and ultimately so did the team, but in the end, he was honored by Heavenly Father in a way that was profound. Yes, it would have been a fairy-tale ending if they won the championship with Dane on the court, but it would not have had the impact it did on everyone if it had not ended the way it did.

Dane will be remembered for his courage to stand up for what he knew to be right, to honor God over man and a game. As a result, he will be remembered by players and coaches long after the best games and players have faded from memory over time. Most importantly, Dane came to know that if we honor God, He will honor us in His own way and time. The standard works teach this doctrine resoundingly:

> Wherefore the Lord God of Israel saith, I said indeed that thy house, and the house of thy father, should walk before me forever: but now the Lord saith, Be it far from me; for them that honour me I will honour, and they that despise me shall be lightly esteemed. (1 Samuel 2:30)

> The fear of the Lord is the instruction of wisdom; and before honour is humility. (Proverbs 15:33)

> If any man serve me, let him follow me; and where I am, there shall also my servant be: if any man serve me, him will my Father honour. (John 12:26)

> For thus saith the Lord—I, the Lord, am merciful and gracious unto those who fear me, and delight to honor those who serve me in righteousness and in truth unto the end. (D&C 76:5)

Take your pick, it does not matter; they all clearly teach how God delights to honor those who honor Him. Make no mistake, honoring God and Christ requires sacrifice, and it is never comfortable or convenient.

We must remember that the crowd is not more important than the Creator. When we learn to put God and Christ first in our lives, then those difficult choices are not tough because of what we give up, but hard because we know that some will not understand. Once we make those tough decisions, we will come to know clearly that we made the right choice when we are honored openly in uniquely packaged ways by others for our example. Choose God over a game, and you will always win the match.

Principle to Live By

When we honor our Heavenly Father and His Son Jesus Christ openly at our own expense, we will be openly honored by God in ways that also bring the respect of others because of our example.

28

An Inconvenient Impression

Following the Spirit can be a life-defining moment

After being married for several years, I was called to teach early-morning seminary for high school–aged students. That is a difficult thing to do, as anyone who has taught seminary knows. Most classes begin somewhere between 5:30 and 6:30 a.m., and it is an amazing experience to watch the dedication of these young people who voluntarily get up that early to start their day studying the scriptures before heading to school.

I remember going to early-morning "cemetery" myself, as the kids call it, and can't believe I wanted to go, but if I am honest, I went because of a cute girl who attended a rival high school, and that was the only time I would get to see her. The funny and yet aggravating thing was she hardly ever came, but I did not want to miss a day in case she showed up. As a result, I ended up graduating.

My second year of teaching, I was approached by the full-time coordinator of that seminary program, and he asked if I would consider teaching full time as a career. I think my first reaction was to laugh and say something cryptic because I knew what that would require. At that time, those full-time religious educators only had ten-month contracts, they didn't get paid much, and they had to move about every three to five years to fill other assignments. I knew this because I would work painting for some of the full-time institute directors in the summer as they tried to augment their income, and that lifestyle did not appeal to me. Over a two-year period, they asked me multiple times, and I refused each time without hesitation.

After college, I started to work in business, and regardless of my efforts, every three to five years I found myself looking for another job because of downsizing or lack of mobility and growth opportunities.

Now I was forty years old and working for a self-funding medical benefits company as a vice president of administration. We would help companies and professionals provide medical and dental benefits for their employees and then manage everything for them. I liked the work, the owners, and the people I worked for, but it just did not feel like a long-term career for me. One day I received word that the owner was going to sell the company or close it down and retire. Again, I was looking at having to find another job within the next six months. The owner's son and I were now responsible to deal with the clients and employees and the impending change.

I was serving in a bishopric at the time and attended a training meeting one evening with an authority of the Church. I clearly remember sitting down after visiting with friends and then out of the blue having a subtle impression to talk to a friend of mine who was also serving in a bishopric and who was a full-time employee of the Church Education System. I thought to myself, *Why*? He was a friend, but as I looked around, he was not there when the meeting started so I blew off the thought. Again, as I was listening to instruction from an authority of the Church, I had a stronger impression to talk to my friend, and then he showed up to the meeting. I still did not know why.

It was now almost impossible for me to concentrate and listen in a meaningful way to the instruction being given because my mind was occupied with the continual thoughts to talk to my friend, along with wondering why I needed to do that. I never got an answer, just the impression to do so.

Following the meeting, I approached my friend and we exchanged our friendly pleasantries and then he asked me directly how work was going. It wasn't a casual inquiry but a pointed question. I told him that I was going to be out of work soon and needed to find another career, but I did not have much time to do so because we were in the middle of downsizing the company with the idea to sell it or shut it down. He just said to me, "You should be in CES." I replied that I thought I was too old, and in fact I had turned it down emphatically fifteen years earlier. He said it did not matter and shared with me that during the meeting he kept getting impressions to talk to me. Now the Lord had my attention, and I was interested in where this was going.

My friend and I talked for a short time, and he told me I needed to ask for a release from my current calling and begin teaching early morning seminary again, which would start in a few weeks. He explained the evaluation process I would have to go through that might take a couple of years. I don't know why, but I felt like I needed to do this even though it did not sound reasonable on any level. On the way home, I offered a heartfelt prayer desiring to know if this was the Lord's will for me and my family, and I had a powerful witness, followed by a sweet peaceful feeling that all would be well.

When I got home, I told my wife and she was very supportive. I then called my stake president and asked for a release, to which he said no because they needed me where I was currently serving. I explained it was a career move for me and my family, and he finally relented. I started teaching several weeks later, and eventually I was hired as an institute director and coordinator of multiple stakes of early morning seminary in Los Angeles. This would require a move for me and my family, and it would not be easy.

It was not as simple as I just described; in fact, it was miraculous in how it happened, but all that really matters is that I followed that impression and it changed the direction of my life. The lesson may seem obvious, but it is another thing altogether to follow impressions when they come, when they are not reasonable or convenient.

I am now close to retiring with over twenty-two years of a wonderful, stable career and a comfortable future ahead. I am amazed at how the Lord works in quiet yet profound ways in our lives. I am forever grateful for following that impression without knowing any details and thankful for a friend who did the same.

That was not the first time nor the last that I have had impressions that I have followed that have led to impactful moments in my life. But it was one of the most defining moments of my life and has ultimately impacted thousands of people besides me and my family.

Like many of you, we receive impressions daily and, if followed, they may simply make our day a little smoother, bless the lives of others in small but significant ways, or in some cases may lead to defining moments that change the course of our lives forever. The great challenge at times is to recognize those impressions and be willing to follow them even if they are not reasonable or convenient.

Those impressions are simply revelation. Though they can be subtle, they are confirmed in a powerful way if we embrace them. We find a great description of this process of receiving revelation in the Doctrine and Covenants:

> Yea, behold, I will tell you in your mind and in your heart, by the Holy Ghost, which shall come upon you and which shall dwell in your heart.
>
> Now, behold, this is the spirit of revelation; behold, this is the spirit by which Moses brought the children of Israel through the Red Sea on dry ground. (D&C 8:2–3)

The Lord provides a dual witness: the mind and the heart. The mind is the reasonable part of the witness, and the heart is the general or emotional aspect. Sometimes we get a feeling to do something, and when we act on those feelings, we receive more specific guidance. Other times, we may receive very specific thoughts, and when we act upon those, we receive a general feeling of assurance that we are doing the right thing. There is no rigid or specific order of how this works; both can come at the same time.

What is interesting to me is what is taught in verse 3. Why does the Lord throw Moses in there? When we contemplate the circumstances that Moses found himself in with the children of Israel reacting to the armies of Egypt coming upon them, we might ask ourselves what that looks like and sound like. It must have been pandemonium. How does one receive revelation under those crazy circumstances?

The important thing for me is knowing that Moses received saving instructions in the same way we receive revelation; it came to his mind and heart. In this instance, how reasonable does parting the sea sound? But the witness to the heart of confirming feelings make things that sound unreasonable feel appropriate. I think one of the messages of verse 3 is that we receive revelation the same way a prophet does, even in dire circumstances, when it sounds most unreasonable, but if we respond we too can be delivered in miraculous ways. I love that idea! Truly the Lord is no respecter of persons, and He does love all of us.

In my situation, it was not a spectacular experience with a visible miracle performed. Yet, over time, when looking back over the course of my life, it has produced miraculous blessings and opportunities for me, my family, and so many others.

I believe these subtle impressions come daily, and if we will be receptive to them and respond in kind, we will witness miracles in our lives and the lives of those we love. I appreciate the Lord's invitation and promise:

> Therefore, let your hearts be comforted concerning Zion; for all flesh is in mine hands; be still and know that I am God. (D&C 101:16)

> Therefore, dearly beloved brethren, let us cheerfully do all things that lie in our power; and then may we stand still, with the utmost assurance, to see the salvation of God, and for his arm to be revealed. (D&C 123:17)

Both passages have a specific context for which they are used, but the inherent truth is the same and applicable to our subject. We must learn to be quiet and still inside to hear the Spirit whisper to us thoughts and impressions that will require us to respond before the Lord can work in our behalf in simple and yet profound ways. I know the Lord's goodness in this way and bear witness He can be an everyday Savior for you and me if we allow Him to do so. I am so grateful I responded to His invitation when it did not seem reasonable to me at that moment but became clearer as time passed.

Principle to Live By

Learn to be still enough inside to recognize impressions when they come, and then learn to respond to them even when they do not make sense at first. Then watch the Lord work in our lives in miraculous ways.

29

A Man Lying on the Side of the Road

Keep responding to the Spirit

At one point in my life, I worked for a cable company as an installer and technician. This kind of work was hard and grueling, especially in the summer months. Back then, we often had to climb telephone poles using a technique called gaffing. This required you to strap a sharp metal spike to the inside of your legs, and then, with a belt wrapped around the pole, you walk up the pole by slamming the spike into the wood while sliding the belt up the pole as you moved. It was a little scary and very taxing to climb twenty-five to thirty feet up a pole this way, and scary to stay up there as you worked. After connecting the cable to the junction box, we would also crawl into attics and under homes to install the cable to the television. After a day of crawling and climbing you would be covered with sweat, dirt, and spiderwebs. It was mostly miserable work.

About this time in my life, I was trying to be more receptive to spiritual impressions, and sure enough, I started to receive impressions that I would try to follow, but usually nothing happened. This continued for weeks and then months—not every day but weekly and sometimes more. It became frustrating to follow an impression and then have nothing that I could identify happen. I eventually started to question myself, and again, my ability to receive revelation. I felt like I was just creating these impressions or feelings within myself. Maybe you have experienced something similar.

Then, one hot late summer afternoon, as I was heading home from a long hard day, I had the impression to drive home in a way that I normally did not take. It wasn't out of the way; it just was not the most direct way I was used to taking. I was hot and sweaty, tired, itchy, hungry, and just not in the mood to do something that I was sure would lead to nothing. As I got closer to home, I had a more profound impression to take the road that I did not want to take. As I approached the turn off, I suddenly turned onto that road. The road eventually came to an incline that veered to the left as you drove up the hill. As I drove about halfway up, my eyes caught a glimpse of a man laying facedown with his head pointing downhill on the side of the road. I was stunned and quickly turned into the nearest driveway and ran over to the man. He was an older gentleman who had apparently fallen, and he had been there a while because blood had flowed about five or six feet down the hill and pooled. I tried to find a pulse but couldn't detect one and found he was cold to the touch. I turned him over to see if he was breathing but also could not sense that he was. Suddenly the neighbor whose driveway I had parked in came over and asked what was going on, and I told her to go call an ambulance and paramedic. She took off, and I turned my attention back to the man.

I could not detect life in the man, and I started to get a sick feeling inside when a strong impression came that I needed to give this man a blessing. My first thoughts were, *I'm alone, I don't have consecrated oil with me*, and *How would this make a difference if he is already dead?* Again, but more forcefully came the impression to just lay my hands on the man's head and bless him to survive. I placed my dirty sweat- and creosol-covered hands on his head and gave him a priesthood blessing that he would survive and be healed to return to his family.

When I said "Amen," the man made a sound and moved, and I was shocked and stood up just as the ambulance came along with a fire truck and paramedics. These professionals took over immediately and I just walked back to my car without saying a word to anyone. I drove home quietly, thinking about what had just happened. I did not have time to process it or understand it when it was happening, but now I was trying to take in the significance of what I just experienced with that old man. Suddenly I wasn't hungry, tired, or uncomfortable in any way; I was just surprised and dumbfounded. I thought about what might have happened if I had not gone that way home. I pondered, *Was the man dead? How long had he been there? What caused him to fall? Why hadn't anyone else seen him or stopped to help?* I just had a flood of questions stream into my mind.

Later on that night, I called the nearest hospital to see if an older man with a face and head injury found on the side of the road had been admitted. I did not know his name or anything about him, except that I had seen him a few times walking in the area but always alone. The hospital finally figured out who I was talking about, and they said he was in stable condition and doing okay.

Several months later, when on my way home from another long day of work, I felt impressed to go home that way again, and I was hoping I wasn't going to find another person or that same old gentleman on the side of the road again. However, I saw that same man walking with a companion holding onto his arm. What a rush as the Spirit washed over me as I kept driving on, thinking how wonderful it was that he was able to get back to his life and what he loved to do. What a tender mercy for me as well.

As I pondered that experience, I was grateful that I responded, even when it wasn't convenient or comfortable, and especially since it felt unreasonable for me to do so after having so many other impressions in the past months that produced nothing. I started to feel that perhaps the Lord was testing my faithfulness so when a significant need arose He knew I would respond. It was interesting for me to consider how that man wasn't someone important to me; he was an older man with not too many years left, and he wasn't a member of the Church who would even understand what a priesthood blessing was. Yet the Lord in love and mercy felt it was important that he was found, administered unto, and restored for His own divine reasons. It is not important for me to know why. Rather, I just need to know that it happened because it was the Lord's will. Remember my experience with blessing the squirrel? What a different outcome!

There are times in our lives when we are being tested and prepared long in advance of a defining moment for us and for others. A couple of scriptures come to mind that I believe have application here:

> And we will prove them herewith, to see if they will do all things whatsoever the Lord their God shall command them;
>
> And they who keep their first estate shall be added upon; and they who keep not their first estate shall not have glory in the same kingdom with those who keep their first estate; and they who keep their second estate shall have glory added upon their heads for ever and ever. (Abraham 3:25–26)

From these teachings to Abraham, we learn that being proven worthy is a pattern that was active in the pre-mortal life. And we know that it is the Lord's pattern here in mortality:

> For he will give unto the faithful line upon line, precept upon precept; and I will try you and prove you herewith. (D&C 98:12)

The Lord leads and teaches us in increments, based upon our knowledge and abilities, through a process of time to prove to Him, and I suppose to ourselves, that we can be trusted for further and greater things. This requires us to be patient with the Lord and ourselves as we are being tutored in ways much higher than our own abilities to understand. Sometimes it just doesn't make sense, and yet it always makes sense as we look back on it.

I not only believe, but now more clearly understand, why it is important for us to not only learn to respond to the impressions we receive, but to never stop responding simply because we feel nothing significant occurs. The Lord may be preparing us for a time when it is extremely significant, even life changing, for us to be counted worthy and trustworthy enough to be where the Lord needs us to be at a given moment to bless the lives of others. The Lord's preparation is as important as the Lord's desired outcome for us and others. Don't stop responding; we may need one another in a moment of significance.

Principle to Live By

Learning to respond to spiritual impressions is not enough; we must be willing to respond even when nothing occurs. As we do so, we prove ourselves trustworthy to respond in moments that may be life changing for us and others.

30

Skiing with My Wife

Avoiding fear and self-centeredness

I am a very bad skier. Why? Because I am too worried about how others perceive my skiing abilities, rather than just putting in the time and effort to become better. I once unintentionally set a distance record for skiing backward on one ski because I was too proud to go down. I have skied through trees, over rocks, into restricted areas, and more. I once turned in a pair of rented skies that had so many groves on the bottom that I was sure I was going to have to buy them; they were so badly damaged. But my wife—she can ski.

The first time my wife and I went skiing together, she found out how bad I was before we even got off the lift and onto the slopes. As we were riding up the lift, all I was worried about was getting off the chair without falling and making a scene. I was so preoccupied with fear for a moment that had not happened yet, and I just got more nervous by the second. I kept telling my wife, and each time more forcefully, "Don't touch me in any way as we are getting off the lift." I could not express it clearly enough how she was not to cause me to lose my balance under any circumstances. I was determined not to go down in front of everyone.

It happened to be a crowded day and every chair was full, so if you made a mistake, you were not only going down in humiliation, you were going to frustrate everyone else as the lift had to be stopped so you could crawl out of the way, or have people drag you out of the way. I just kept seeing myself sprawled out on the snow and it just got worse in my mind. By now I was breathing heavy and sweating in the cold.

My wife kept reassuring me everything would be okay and to just relax, but for some reason I just could not let go of the thoughts and feelings of my potential humiliation waiting for me. I continued to frustrate myself and my wife with my adamant instructions to the point of causing her some anxiety that something bad was about to happen. She told me to stop talking about it and just relax, but I couldn't. It was the longest ride of my life and I started to get a sick feeling in the pit of my stomach; it was worse than pre-game jitters.

As we approached the moment of truth, one last time I said to my wife, "Don't touch me!" As our skies hit the snow and we stood up, I lost my balance and automatically reached out with my right hand as a reflex, grabbed my wife by the jacket just below her neck, and tried to restore my balance. I slapped her coat so hard it made a loud sound, and if no one was looking originally, now their attention was drawn to the guy who was aggressively attacking a woman getting off the lift.

My wife was too light to counteract my off-balance weight and so I started winging her around like a rag doll trying to stay upright. We are now going down the incline from the chair and I am holding on to her and swinging her back and forth until I threw her down in the snow with great force, and then held up my arms above my head in triumph that I was still standing. Yea, that's right, I did it—I did not go down in front of everyone and I was so proud of myself.

As I turned around to see where my wife was, expecting her to revel in my accomplishment, I first saw the lift guy looking at me with disdain as others were glaring at me as if I were a jerk, some smirking, others laughing, and a few even looked angry. As I looked back toward the lift, there was my wife facedown in the snow with people trying to help her up. As she got to her feet, she said with emphasis and appropriate sarcasm—"Don't touch me!" Oh man, I knew I was in trouble, and I knew I deserved it.

I felt terrible, but it did not matter at that point how badly I felt or how sorry I was; I had physically assaulted my wife in public and humiliated her in front of everyone. She did not ski with me down the run and I did not blame her. To make things worse, I assaulted several other people on my way down the run because I was so out of control. Not surprisingly, we have never been skiing together again.

So what did I learn from that experience? Well, a couple of things. First, from a literal perspective, never go skiing again. Secondly, from a spiritual perspective, don't be so self-centered. But before I develop the idea of self-centeredness, I want to touch on the idea of fear. Over the years, I have come to realize that I manifested something so many people experience in life: fear of things that have not happened yet. People are fearful of upcoming exams, marriage, having children, getting a job, being able to own a home, and wondering how they will be able to retire. Like me on the lift, I was so fearful of something that had not yet happened that I became preoccupied with myself and a potential future event.

If we are not careful, we become so fearful of the future that we can in some cases enhance and maybe even ensure that our fears are realized. Fear and faith cannot exist at the same moment in an individual; one must overcome the other, and we choose which one wins.

I paraphrase a line I once heard in a movie, that a person who cannot believe in something by faith is doomed to live a life dominated by doubt. Doubt leads to fear, and fear causes failure—failure to try and failure to believe. Speaking about signs of the last days and the condition of the earth that could bring fear, the Lord said:

> And also cometh the testimony of the voice of thunderings, and the voice of lightnings, and the voice of tempests, and the voice of the waves of the sea heaving themselves beyond their bounds.
>
> And all things shall be in commotion; and surely, men's hearts shall fail them; for fear shall come upon all people. (D&C 88:90–91)

We can spend our lives in fear of things that have not happened yet, or we can be hopeful, prepare ourselves to meet future challenges with a positive attitude, and then do our best to bring about a desired result. When we do slip and fall, we get back up and move forward with faith that we will succeed the next time we get off the lift into a slippery experience. And just because we may go down doesn't mean we need to take others down with us.

Now onto another lesson learned. I learned that my negative preoccupation with a future event caused me to be very selfish and self-centered. I was so preoccupied with myself that I caused greater anxiety in myself and in my wife. In a short ride I became so prideful, arrogant, and selfish that I never once thought about making sure my wife got off the lift safely. I harassed her all the way up the lift and then accosted her as we got off the lift just to make sure I did not look bad in front of others. Even worse, I celebrated my pathetic victory because I was still standing while she was facedown in the snow. I was ashamed, not because of my poor skiing abilities, but because it revealed my selfish and self-centered nature in such a glaring way and so openly. This is opposite of what Paul taught about charity—the pure love of Christ. Notice one of the characteristics of charity:

> Doth not behave itself unseemly, seeketh not her own, is not easily provoked, thinketh no evil. (1 Corinthians 13:5)

Charity is selfless and is manifested in serving others and their interests, even when our needs are real and pressing. Selfish tendencies are of the natural man. I love the idea that we cannot keep the first great commandment to love God without keeping the second commandment to love our fellow man.

> And behold, I tell you these things that ye may learn wisdom; that ye may learn that when ye are in the service of your fellow beings ye are only in the service of your God. (Mosiah 2:17)

Because serving others is serving God, we must diminish in self-centeredness and grow in love, and this is a manifestation of the spiritual gift of charity. Pure love is the key to overcoming the selfish and self-centered tendencies of the natural man. This kind of love can only come from the Savior, who is the greatest manifestation of God's love for His children. Christ is the perfect example of this kind of selfless love and service for the welfare of others more than Himself.

My selfish desires to avoid humiliation on the ski lift did nothing to magnify myself, even though I remained upright; to the contrary, it humiliated me even more because of how I treated someone I loved, and how it was perceived by others. Further, it affected the trip down the hill and every day since that day because my wife will never step on a snow-packed mountain with me ever again. What a cost to pay just for me to remain standing as I got off the lift!

In our daily trips on the lifts of life, we must learn to look outside of ourselves and be mindful of others who may have similar or even more anxious concerns than we do and find ways to help them. In the process, we help ourselves, and together we can help each other remain upright and standing in our challenging moments without being humiliated by things we say or do that are selfish and self-centered. Standing together brings balance to our lives.

Principle to Live By

Learn to be more selfless and less selfish. When we have anxious concerns for ourselves, stop and look around to see if there is someone else who may need our help, and be willing to put others first. Then God will make us a priority for His help and strength.

31

A Ball, a Street Gutter, and a Drunk Indian

Judging others righteously

When I was about six or seven, we lived on the edge of the county, with wide open spaces east of us. Not far from us was an Indian reservation, and we would occasionally see Native Americans around the area. I can't ever remember having a problem with them, but there were some rumors flying around that there were "drunk Indians" around who would attack or kidnap children. These were quietly whispered rumors, and all the kids were aware of it. It is amazing that no matter where you go, in every community, rumors arise, most of which are false, but they get circulated as if they are true and it causes division, unrighteous judgment, and enmity between people.

In our community, kids were always playing in the neighborhood and beyond and never once saw what was rumored. We would be running and riding all over the area and would often play ball in the street and always felt safe. My brother and I would play baseball or throw the football around and find that the neighborhood kids would come running to join in on the fun; it was great being a kid back then, and we always felt safe and free.

The only real problem for us with playing in the street was the gutters. You still see them now and then in older neighborhoods, an opening about two or three feet wide on the curb, where water would flow into heading to the sewer system to keep the streets clear. Between the street and the sidewalk was a concrete slab with a manhole cover so they could go down into the chamber using metal handles to climb on. I never saw anyone go down in one, but I thought about doing it a couple of times if I could only lift the heavy round metal manhole cover.

When water ran down the gutter into the chamber, it sounded like a trickling creek from people watering lawns or washing cars. After a rain, it would really sound like a waterfall as water dropped down about three or four feet into a drainage system. We were always told the water ran all the way to the coast and emptied into the ocean. We were commanded never to go in there because it would wash us away out to sea. Parents!

Kids will be kids, however, and we discovered if you stuck your head in sideways you could see down into the drop and all the stuff that would accumulate at the bottom. The echo in the chamber was really fun and we would stick our heads in and yell things so we could listen to the reverberating sounds.

One of our reoccurring problems we would face when throwing around the baseball in the street was that it would sometimes get away from us and roll to the gutter heading for the opening. At times, if it was swallowed by the opening, we had to crawl halfway in the hole while someone held our legs so one of us could try to reach down and retrieve the ball. It didn't happen that often but it was enough that we became proficient at ball retrievals from the "gutter hole," as we called it.

One afternoon it was just me and my brother playing catch together and a missed ball went down the hole. We just reacted instinctually; I climbed halfway into the opening and my brother knelt down, grabbing my calves while I stretched for the ball. I kept inching forward a little more until the middle of my thighs were to the edge of the opening—if my brother let go I did not have enough body weight to hold me up and I would tumble into the hole head first. But I trusted him to hold on.

As I inched forward and was reaching for the ball, my brother suddenly let go of one leg and let out a whimpering sound. I slipped sideways and put my hand on the wall below me to try and prop myself up so I would not fall in. I was able to use my stomach muscles to pull my torso up and turn my head to the side to see with one eye some legs staggering toward me and my brother. Suddenly my brother let go of the other leg and ran, and I just knew it was a drunk Indian coming to push me into the gutter hole and send me to the ocean where I would be lost forever. I was trying to hold myself up by lifting up one leg to the top of the gutter hole while pushing against the wall below me when suddenly two hands grabbed my ankles just as I was slipping into the hole. I screamed and then I was yanked out of the opening, banging my head a bit because I did not turn it sideways fast enough while coming out. It happened so fast and I thought I was toast.

The man pulled me out and turned me over, kneeling above me with his face inches from mine, but I couldn't make out his features because the sun was right behind him. I didn't know what he was going to do and could not tell by his demeanor if he had bad intensions. I was just scared and thought maybe I was going to be kidnapped. Shockingly he just leaned forward and said, "You shouldn't be playing in the gutter, boy." What I remember was that his breath was horrible, and I thought it had to be from booze.

As he stood up, he grabbed me by my shoulders and lifted me up. I could now see he was an older Native American man with bad teeth. He then turned and walked away in a halting manner. I stood there shocked and relieved at the same time that he did not kill me or kidnap me—instead he saved me! What was that all about?

As I stood there and watched him walk away I realized what I thought was a drunk Indian staggering toward us was actually an old man with a limp. I totally misjudged the man, but as a boy with rumors swirling around in my head, I pictured him as described and was sure that he was going to do something horrible to me. My fears were enhanced by the fact that my brother fled, thinking the same thing, and I was stuck in a very precarious position. Yet the truth was that I was totally wrong. I let rumors and stories feed my prejudice until I believed them, even though I had never seen any evidence or even knew of anyone who had witnessed or experienced anything described in the rumors.

I not only misjudged the man's intentions, I misjudged the man. Concerning judgment, the scriptures teach:

> Ye shall do no unrighteousness in judgment: thou shalt not respect the person of the poor, nor honour the person of the mighty: but in righteousness shalt thou judge thy neighbour. (Leviticus 19:15)

The scriptures do not teach that we are not to judge people or situations, but rather to do so righteously. Our very existence requires that we judge; the challenge is to learn how to do so appropriately. So how does one learn to judge righteously in a world so full of enmity and hatred toward one another socially, politically, ethnically, and religiously? The Lord throws further light on the subject:

> And now, verily, verily, I say unto thee, put your trust in that Spirit which leadeth to do good yea, to do justly, to walk humbly, to judge righteously; and this is my Spirit.
>
> Verily, verily, I say unto you, I will impart unto you of my Spirit, which shall enlighten your mind, which shall fill your soul with joy. (D&C 11:12–13)

It is the influence of the Spirit that will enlighten our minds and focus our mind's eye, allowing us to see and judge correctly. The Spirit comes by faith and humility, principles that help us set aside the world's wisdom and judge things from a loftier perspective, rather than worldly driven judgments flowing from emotion and passion.

The Savior is the perfect example of this when He was confronted by individuals trying to trap Him on the law of adultery:

> And early in the morning he came again into the temple, and all the people came unto him; and he sat down, and taught them.
>
> And the scribes and Pharisees brought unto him a woman taken in adultery; and when they had set her in the midst,
>
> They say unto him, Master, this woman was taken in adultery, in the very act.
>
> Now Moses in the law commanded us, that such should be stoned: but what sayest thou?
>
> This they said, tempting him, that they might have to accuse him. But Jesus stooped down, and with his finger wrote on the ground, as though he heard them not.
>
> So when they continued asking him, he lifted up himself, and said unto them, He that is without sin among you, let him first cast a stone at her.
>
> And again he stooped down, and wrote on the ground.
>
> And they which heard it, being convicted by their own conscience, went out one by one, beginning at the eldest, even unto the last: and Jesus was left alone, and the woman standing in the midst.
>
> When Jesus had lifted up himself, and saw none but the woman, he said unto her, Woman, where are those thine accusers? hath no man condemned thee?
>
> She said, No man, Lord. And Jesus said unto her, Neither do I condemn thee: go, and sin no more. (John 8:2–11)

There are several important contextual things to understand here, the first being that only the woman was brought before the Lord. Where is the man? This reveals the intentions of the crowd as they bring the issue to the Lord, for the woman is the instrument to bait the Lord. Secondly, the Savior had not come to judge the people at this time but rather to save the people through His atoning sacrifice. Judgment comes when Christ returns. Here, the Lord in His challenge to the people as to who should cast the first stone places judgment at their own feet. He does not judge them but initiates the need for self-judgment. Still further, when it comes to the woman, the Lord does not forgive her, but says that He does not condemn her with the injunction to go and sin no more. What an example of righteous judgment!

As mortals, we are so preoccupied with a prescribed punishment for certain behavior and may even convict a person in our own minds before we even meet them, witness any evidence that judgment is required, or characterize in our conversations a prejudiced view of them because of what is swirling around in rumors.

Fortunately for us, Christ looked at that woman the same way He looks at us, from the perspective of our divine potential. He does clearly identify the course back to that divine potential for the woman, by telling her not to sin that way again. He did not diminish the severity of the sin; rather He magnified the woman's potential to be better. It was not just a commandment to go and sin no more; it was a statement of truth that she could do it.

The Indian man who I misjudged all those years ago still creeps into my life, through other people, as I still struggle at times because of how media portrays others from a totally different and skewed perspective. If I am not careful, I can still characterize people of a different persuasion than myself to be wrong, stupid, deceived, or just flat-out evil designing people. Do they exist? Absolutely! Does everyone who expresses their beliefs in a similar way deserve to be judged as others who manifest those tendencies? No way!

Righteous judgment requires an influence that is not of this world. It requires the influence of the Spirit and not the media or rumor, so we can see clearly what is real and important. To this day, I don't know if that man who pulled me from the gutter was staggering from drink or just limping from an injury and old age. I don't know if his breath was bad from booze or his rotten teeth. All I know is he was an Indian and he saved me from possible injury out of what I believe to be a genuine concern for a young boy in a dangerous situation. I hope to meet that man on the other side, so I can judge him for who he really was and see him for who he really will be in the eternities. Careful judgment is righteous judgment.

Principle to Live By

Learn to judge righteously by the Spirit and not by emotion, passion, or rumor. Then we will see people from the perspective of their divine potential as the Lord sees them and for who they truly are.

32

A Baptism, a Blessing, and a Sealing All in the Same Day

The Lord blesses everyone personally in a shared moment

My daughter Shea is adopted. After Dane was born, we tried for another seven years to have another child and then were blessed to adopt our daughter. This age difference made for an interesting possibility as Dane reached eight years old and was ready for baptism. Because Tina and I were sealed in the temple, Dane was born under the covenant and therefore automatically sealed to us. However, Shea came to us around six months old, so she would need to be sealed to us after the adoption. We looked forward to giving Shea a name and a blessing for the records of the Church, to Dane's baptism, and to Shea being sealed to us, but we did not anticipate the potential challenges from the timing of these things happening.

As Dane was approaching his eighth birthday, we started to plan for his baptism, and we just assumed he could be baptized on any Saturday convenient for us as a family. We would schedule the event on a weekend that would allow for all extended family to be there and would make the program a family affair. As we shared our plans with our local priesthood and auxiliary leaders, we found out that our stake did not do individual baptisms but rather did one a month on an assigned weekend with other children and their families of our stake. We were instructed that those leaders who had stewardship over the stake baptisms would oversee the program details.

Our first reaction was one of disappointment and confusion. What is the big deal about having a personal experience as a family on such an important day for our son? As we whined a bit about our lack of control over our son's special day, we came to understand that it is an ordinance which needs to be presided over by a member of the bishopric and put on by the stake Primary organization under the direction of the assigned high councilor over stake baptisms. It makes sense that it has to be organized in a way that is also convenient for those who have callings to attend and preside. After all, if everyone were allowed to plan their own program, hold it when they wanted and where they wanted, it would be total chaos and nearly impossible for those who have a specific stewardship to be able to attend each one.

As we started to plan according to the scheduled weekend for our stake baptisms, we realized we still had an unusual circumstance that needed special attention, permission, and preparation for our specific needs. We needed to schedule Shea's naming and blessing, and then her sealing to us. It was not feasible to do these things on different weekends and expect family and friends to attend when some would be traveling a great distance to be there. We needed to consider how we could do all these things on the same weekend when it would be convenient for everyone. And it would all have to happen after our court appearance to make the adoption final.

As we considered our situation, we realized that things started to align in terms of timing and availability for these three things to happen on the same day, allowing everyone to be there. As we approached our priesthood leaders, they could see our unusual circumstance and were willing to help us make this happen. We were given permission to have Dane's baptism on a different Saturday than the stake baptisms if there was another child to be baptized, so it did not appear we were receiving preferential treatment. It just happened that some close friends also had been planning their son's baptism for the same month, and so we asked them if they would be willing to combine our programs together, and then have them participate in the other activities of that day with us. They agreed and were excited to do this with us.

Now that the baptism was set, we had to plan the naming and blessing of Shea, which required our local leaders to attend and preside over this non-saving ordinance. We asked if it could happen right after the baptisms, so the priesthood leaders would already be there. We also needed to clear the names of all those who would participate. Finally, we needed the bishop of our ward to give Dane an interview for his limited-use recommend so he could go into the temple with us for the sealing of Shea to our family. This would also have to follow the baptisms and blessing. All of this was approved as well, and we felt good about how things were working out.

Lastly, we needed to get approval from the temple to have Shea's sealing to us on that same day and at a time after the baptisms and blessing that would give us all enough time to get over there and prepare for the sealing. Wow, what a nightmare, but miraculously the timing and scheduling and attendance of family and friends all fell into place. The date was set for May 31, 1996.

For weeks leading up to that day, and on that day, there were so many details that could have become such a distraction from the significance of the special events that would take place. Our heads were swimming, and we were full of hope and anxiety that everything would go smoothly and would be convenient and comfortable for family and friends, because it would be a long day of rushing around.

How unusual to have a baptism, a blessing, and a sealing all in the same day. Almost lost in all of this was how special it was for Dane to be allowed to go into the temple sealing room as an eight-year-old, newly baptized member of the Church, and witness the sealing of his sister to our family. Amazingly, all our family, extended family, and friends were able to attend all or part of the day's activities, and three generations of priesthood holders were there to participate—it truly was a special day.

Now let me share some special details that will open the door to several important lessons we learned from that experience. I had the privilege of baptizing my son, and then giving my daughter a name and a blessing. I was excited and focused on exercising my priesthood appropriately to honor Heavenly Father and the Lord and access promised blessings for us as a family. I was grateful things went smoothly, and as I was pondering upon how well things turned out, my son shared with his mother and me what kind of an experience he had as I immersed him under the water.

Dane said that as his face was covered with water he had a vision open in his mind where he saw John the Baptist baptizing Jesus Christ. He saw it clearly and said it made him feel warm all over. What a special experience for an eight-year-old boy to have, and we were grateful he shared that with us. My pleasure came after the witnesses nodded in approval, and I felt a special warmth as I embraced my son in the font. Two different perspectives with two different outcomes, both good but one more profound than the other.

Later that day, my father, who served as one of the two witnesses to ensure the ordinance was done appropriately, shared with me that when Dane went under the water he saw in his mind the Savior's baptism by John. When I shared what Dane had witnessed with my father, we realized a grandpa and a grandson saw the same vision simultaneously. What a special moment for them to connect in such a sacred way. Both visions validated one another and communicated heaven's pleasure for that event.

Following the baptisms, I gave Shea a name and a blessing, with three generations of priesthood holders standing with me. Shea was calm as we all held her and there was a sweet peaceful Spirit there, as my wife and I experienced a deep and abiding feeling that Shea was intended for our family even though she came in an unusual way to be part of it. Tears flowed, and everyone said there was a special feeling there as we participated in this special ordinance designated by the Lord.

When we arrived at the temple, Tina and I dressed into our temple clothes and then went to the sealing room where everyone was waiting. Shea and Dane were brought into the room, both dressed in white. Tina and I knelt at the altar across from one another, Dane stood at the head of the altar, while my mother held Shea in her arms and placed her little hand on ours as the ordinance was performed. Shea just looked at us and smiled. The ordinance was brief but powerful as our daughter was sealed to us and blessings pronounced on her as if she were born under the covenant. Shea's demeanor was calm and serene as if she understood what was happening.

Following the sealing ordinance and while still in the sealing room, our friends who had their son baptized with our son shared a special experience that the wife had. While the sealing ordinance was being performed, she saw an older couple standing behind Dane, looking approvingly upon us and smiling. We don't know who they were or why they were there, except that someone from the other side of the veil had a vested interest in the future of that infant and our family and found great joy in witnessing that sacred event. As we gathered together to eat and to visit and ponder on the events of the day, others shared special experiences that took place at the baptism, the blessing, and the sealing. I didn't quite know what to make of all the experiences shared by so many throughout that day, especially since I didn't experience anything out of the ordinary or unusual. But over the years I have come to learn a couple of things from that day.

One lesson for me is that if we are not careful, we can become so focused on the details that call for our continual attention that we may miss significant experiences that can flow from sacred moments. I love the following example in the scriptures that clarifies this for me:

> Then the king of Syria warred against Israel, and took counsel with his servants, saying, In such and such a place shall be my camp.
>
> And the man of God sent unto the king of Israel, saying, Beware that thou pass not such a place; for thither the Syrians are come down.
>
> And the king of Israel sent to the place which the man of God told him and warned him of, and saved himself there, not once nor twice.
>
> Therefore the heart of the king of Syria was sore troubled for this thing; and he called his servants, and said unto them, Will ye not shew me which of us is for the king of Israel?
>
> And one of his servants said, None, my lord, O king: but Elisha, the prophet that is in Israel, telleth the king of Israel the words that thou speakest in thy bedchamber.
>
> And he said, Go and spy where he is, that I may send and fetch him. And it was told him, saying, Behold, he is in Dothan.
>
> Therefore sent he thither horses, and chariots, and a great host: and they came by night, and compassed the city about.
>
> And when the servant of the man of God was risen early, and gone forth, behold, an host compassed the city both with horses and chariots. And his servant said unto him, Alas, my master! how shall we do?
>
> And he answered, Fear not: for they that be with us are more than they that be with them.
>
> And Elisha prayed, and said, Lord, I pray thee, open his eyes, that he may see. And the Lord opened the eyes of the young man; and he saw: and, behold, the mountain was full of horses and chariots of fire round about Elisha. (2 Kings 6:8–17)

My eyes that day were focused more on what was going on around me that I did not see greater things going on. I had to have my eyes opened by others who saw more clearly the spiritual outpourings that I missed. And yet, the Lord blessed me with moments of peace and warmth to acknowledge that what was being done was acceptable unto Him. I am grateful for the Spirit that I felt, and for the gratification that flowed from the events of that day, but I am more grateful for the spiritual receptiveness of so many others who were open to special experiences that deepened the significance of what occurred for all of us that day.

Another lesson I have come to understand is how the Lord blesses everyone in their own way and according to their own spiritual abilities at a given moment. The Savior can be so personal, even in openly shared moments with others. I love that about Him, and His willingness to bless everyone in some way to acknowledge His pleasure that what we are doing is in harmony with His will and desires for us. The individual experiences give greater value to the collective experience shared by everyone and deepens our love and devotion for our Heavenly Father and His Son.

Principle to Live By

When we can learn to focus less on details that can overwhelm us and be more receptive to the spiritual importance of things we do, we will experience spiritual outpourings that can open our eyes to special experiences that deepen our love for God and Christ.

A Parting Thought

I want to end where I began:

> And behold, all things have their likeness, and all things are created and made to bear record of me, both things which are temporal, and things which are spiritual; things which are in the heavens above, and things which are on the earth, and things which are in the earth, and things which are under the earth, both above and beneath: all things bear record of me. (Moses 6:63)

For me, it is all about how everything points to the Savior. It really is that simple and yet so profound. This gives such meaning to life for me, because if this is true, and I firmly believe that it is, then in my daily walk here in mortality I can find His hand and image in my personal experiences. This makes life exciting and worth living, to experience the good and the bad, and be able to learn from them both. To become better so we can be an influence for good in the lives of others and be counted a blessing as well as a friend.

I believe this for you and for everyone else as well. Look for the lessons in your own life experiences, and then lift others to higher plateaus of spiritual awareness by being an example of living life well because you know Christ is an Everyday Savior. That is my hope for everyone.

Thanks for reading,
Winn Raleigh

Acknowledgment

With appreciation to Alonzo L. Gaskill, an accomplished author and scholar, for his willingness to endorse my writing and give encouragement to me as a new author.

About the Author

Winn Raleigh was born in Anchorage, Alaska, and raised in San Diego, California. He has worked with the Church Education System for over twenty years as an Institute of Religion director and full-time religious educator. This is his first published work. He is not unlike you and many others who have unique experiences in life, but he has the ability to tell a simple story and draw powerful lessons from his experiences that can apply to anyone. Winn is married to Tina (McElroy), and they have two married children all living in Orem, Utah.